# The Literary Works Of James Smetham

## James Smetham

# THE
# LITERARY WORKS

OF

# JAMES SMETHAM

EDITED BY

## WILLIAM DAVIES

London

## MACMILLAN AND CO.

### AND NEW YORK

### 1893

# PREFACE

THIS volume contains the chief literary productions of James Smetham—at least such of them
as are likely to appeal in any wide degree to
the public. Already some account of the writer
of them has been given in the introductory
Memoir to the *Letters of James Smetham*, to
which this volume may be considered supple-
mentary. The essays here reprinted, chiefly
from the *London Quarterly Review*, though they
do not admit of the versatility of his epistolary
correspondence, have that in them which certainly
merits a more permanent place in literature than
the pages of a periodical afford or allow of. The
one upon Sir Joshua Reynolds is undoubtedly
a notable production. Its fine literary style, its
compendious and comprehensive survey, its illus-

trative and well-ordered array of facts, may be said to constitute a model in this style of composition. The essay on William Blake has already secured its acceptance in having been reprinted in part as an addendum to Gilchrist's and Rossetti's *Life of Blake*. Neither is the one on Alexander Smith and his School of writers inferior to the others. Many readers will be glad to be reminded of a page in literary history now almost forgotten, to which the literature of the present time is nevertheless largely indebted for a wider enfranchisement—the induction to a more daring and expansive range. Some of the poems at the end of the volume have been already published with the "Letters." It is thought better, however, to reproduce them here for the sake of completeness. Their power of thought, pictorial treatment, and compressed utterance, give them claims which the judicious reader will assuredly not be slow to appreciate.

W. D.

# CONTENTS

## ESSAYS

## POEMS

# ESSAYS

# I

## SIR JOSHUA REYNOLDS[1]

"EVERYTHING turned out fortunately for Sir
Joshua, from the moment of his birth to the hour
I saw him laid in the earth.  Never was a funeral
of ceremony attended with so much sincere con-
cern by all sorts of people.  The day was favourable, the order not broken or interrupted in the
smallest degree.  Your uncle, who was back in
the procession, was struck motionless at his
entering the great west door.  The body was just
then entering the choir, and the organ began to
open, and the long black train before him produced an astonishing effect on his sensibility, and,
considering how dear to him the object of that

[1] This essay was published in the *London Quarterly*,
January 1866, as a review of the " Life and Times of Sir Joshua
Reynolds, by C. Leslie and T. Taylor."

melancholy pomp had been, everything, I think, was just as our deceased friend would, if living, have wished it to be; for he was, as you know, not altogether indifferent to this kind of observance."

No; for though "the sufficiency of Christian immortality frustrates all earthly glory, and the quality of either state after death makes a folly of posthumous memory, yet man is a noble animal, splendid in ashes, and pompous in the grave; solemnising nativities and deaths with equal lustre, nor omitting ceremonies of bravery even in the infamy of his nature."

Two mighty pens—the one in the hand of Edmund Burke, the other in that of Sir Thomas Browne — here supply a solemn and splendid image, and a profound and most eloquent reflection. Both the image and the reflection naturally awaken a strong curiosity to know the whole story of what we may name *The Fortunate Life*, ended and crowned by those dark honours of the sepulchre which he who received them did not hold to be "supervacuous," in this respect not resembling Horace, between whose character and his there were not a few other points of similarity.

This remarkable career was not without record previous to the publication of this biography.

Malone, Northcote, Allan Cunningham, each have
contributed to its illustration; but it has not, till
now, obtained a fair and full expression. Malone's
memoir was slight; Northcote's "pottering" and
illiterate; Allan Cunningham's—in the estimation
of Leslie—was malicious and untrue. Nevertheless, Allan Cunningham's *Lives of the British
Painters, Sculptors, and Architects,* is an entertain-
ing book, giving a lively, and, on the whole, a
truthful impression of the men whom he de-
lineates. He was a poet, and had strong and
glowing sympathy with the various forms of art.
He lived among artists, being for a quarter of a
century foreman to Sir Francis Chantrey, to whom
he gave many a poetic hint. It was he who suggested the lovely idea of the snowdrop in the
hand of the sleeping child in Lichfield Cathedral.
He met constantly with men who knew Reynolds.
He could have, so far as we know, no special
reason for traducing his character. What he
asserts is asserted deliberately, and in his short
memoir of Reynolds there is a note to the effect
that his damaging remarks were made after careful inquiry. It is true that he does not give his
authorities. The impression he leaves on the
reader's mind is a mixed one. Reynolds is placed

before us as a man of high genius and determined
purpose; shrewd, philosophic, equable in temper,
courtly in manners, making and keeping a large
circle of friends among the best classes of his
countrymen for rank, learning, and ability, among
them much beloved, but debarred of court favour
by his independence—all of which agrees with
the record we are about to follow; but he is
exhibited as having another and less pleasing side
to his character, most easily perceived by his
dependants and subordinates, some of whom re-
ported him to be exacting, penurious, and mean.

People "spoke of him," says Allan Cunningham, "as they found him." No explicit contra-
diction or disproof of Cunningham's statements is
given by Leslie. The reader is left to infer from
the evidence before him of the high excellence of
the character of Reynolds—its inconsistency with
the charges brought against him. It is not in
*The British Painters*, however, that we find the
following quotation from Northcote's conversa-
tions; but in Leslie's now published memoir.
"You describe him," said Northcote, "as I remember Baretti once did Sir Joshua at his own
table, saying to him, 'You are extravagant and
mean, generous and selfish, envious and candid,

proud and humble, a genius and a mere ordinary mortal at the same time.' I may not remember his exact words, but that was their effect. *The fact was, that Sir Joshua was a mixed character, like the rest of the world* in that respect; but he knew his own failings, and was on his guard to keep them back as much as possible, though the defects would break out sometimes." Would not Thackeray have taken a careful note of *that?*

The biography before us contains what is likely to be a final and sufficient record of a man who stands out in the front rank of the history of the last century, and who is a conspicuous figure in the Johnsonian circle. All available documents of importance have been gathered and arranged. The pocket-books of the painter have been placed at the disposal of the writers, together with some hitherto unpublished letters and papers, and there is no remaining rumour of untouched stores of information. Leslie's pen has a quiet and unaffected distinctness which seldom becomes smart or glowing, although, where his knowledge as a painter and observer of aspect and manners is brought into play, we are made to feel its subtle charm.

Mr. Taylor has taken up the narrative, left in

a very unfinished state at the death of Leslie, and
by a process of reticulation and addition has completed and put it together in his "own way."
The key to his structural arrangement is found in
a passage of his second volume, where he confesses
his surprise on discovering the *political* complexion of Reynolds's career. This was a fortunate
discovery in more ways than one, for it opens out
a mass of material in the shape of historical
accompaniments, lying within his own power to
execute with spirit, and at the same time wonderfully helps to give importance to the work which,
with much steady, zealous, faithful labour, he has
completed in two good-sized volumes; probably
on the whole more interesting to the general
reader than if Leslie had lived to complete them
himself.

Leslie was, as we all know, an eminent master
in the British School, and lived a placid life in
the pursuit of his favourite art. We know—
although his present coadjutor Mr. Taylor has
published what professes to be his "Autobiography"—far too little about him as a man.
An autobiography that refers as seldom as possible to the author and his doings is not the beau-
ideal of an autobiography, and this is too much

the case with Leslie's. In some gleanings of
recollection in the introduction, we learn that he
did not choose much to visit with any one who
did not care about painting, or did not possess
good specimens; as might therefore be expected,
those portions of the memoir which were prepared
by him are largely professional in material and
tone. We are able to trace with great distinctness the double authorship; Mr. Taylor — he
hardly needed to have done it—has marked off
by square brackets those portions of the work
supplied by himself. The alternations of tone are
noticeable and pleasant. Leslie, a meek and aged
man, plays an air upon his sweet and low-toned
German flute, now tolerably long, now shorter.
But his younger, heartier, more hirsute companion
strikes in suddenly with his *cornet-à-pistons*, wet-
ting his lips and pouring shrill strains from his
instrument, while the timid, apologetic German
flute fills up the pauses. The performers are
admirable friends. The stronger man does not
try to outblow or override the venerable companion over whom he holds the office of protector,
and he allows him a good share of the pence and
praise. The flute dwells doatingly on studio
anecdotes, picture criticisms, mild recollections

and rectifications, culled from Northcote and other sources. The strain is taken up more briskly by the cornet, and the scene shifts to the theatre, the Parliament, the high seas, the club, the gaming-house, the literary coterie, the battle-field, the current scandal, or riot, or duel. When December comes round, year by year, and the deaf president delivers his indistinct, and, as we are here taught to believe, his illogical "dis-course," then the narrator becomes the critic; epitomises and analyses the lecture with in-dependence and good sense, and bows out the year with the list of sitters in the studio of Leicester Square.

Mr. Taylor has some good preliminary quali-fications for work of this sort. He has studied painting closely as a critic, and to some extent practically as a painter. He spent some time entirely among the *ateliers* of Paris, a student himself. He is a poet; he is a dramatist; he is a scholar, and a man of great general accomplish-ments. He is both firm and modest in tone, and cautious in statement. Such of his general picture criticism as we are acquainted with is valuable for its thoughtful and conscientious *fair-ness* and lenity. He has a power of wide appre-

ciation—seldom rises to enthusiasm—does not
vituperate, and does not blunder, and writes with
a painstaking and quiet vivacity which lights up
the page agreeably to the end of the work, leaving
finally on the minds of his readers a very full
and fair impression of the life and times of his
subject.

The lists of sitters, given from the pocket-
books, will have great value as a permanent and
public record to which owners of pictures by Sir
Joshua can appeal for verification, and by which
students of art may trace the progress of Reynolds's
improvement, from the days when he painted the
funny little old children with their dogs and cats,
and lapelled waistcoats, and knee-breeches, and
cocked hats—his own life and fire struggling with
the dullness of the Hudson school—to the days
when he triumphantly swept the dark clouds
round the head of the sublime portrait of Mrs.
Siddons, as the Tragic Muse.

Following the flute and cornet, then, as the
shipwrecked mariners followed the "airy music
and flying noises in the Enchanted Isle" of Pros-
pero, let us trace out some of the lines of life in
this pleasant biography.

July 16, 1723, was the birthday of Joshua

Reynolds. His father was a clergyman. We have
prints of the face of the elder Reynolds from a
picture painted by his son; and Leslie, who seems
to have been deeply touched by the fact, notices
that the costume in that portrait was afterwards
adopted in the charming picture of Oliver Goldsmith, whom Reynolds loved : the same flowing
philosophic robe that suggested the garden and
the porch, the bared neck, the loose, turned-down
collar,—the face in the two pictures being also
seen at the same angle. The features of the
father bear no trace of resemblance to those of
the son. He has a handsomer face, but it has not
the blunt, half-surly expression of the countenance we know so well as " Sir Joshua."

Joshua was not a "marvellous boy." His
father thought him an idle one, as we shall
presently see. He attended his father's school,
and there laid the foundation of such education
as he ever had. How deep that foundation was,
we cannot very exactly judge. We hear nothing
of Greek, and not a great deal of Latin. He read
Ovid more or less in the original, and in after
years, when he had lost the Latin epitaph written
by Dr. Johnson on Goldsmith, the Doctor thought
it possible that Reynolds might recall and re-

write it from memory—"Nil actum reputans dum quid superesset agendum," he writes in 1790 to Sheridan ; and with this scanty amount of material the evidence on that head closes.   A good painter of the Reynolds's organisation is not the man to become a deep scholar.   But he drew in school, if he did not study classics.   On one of these school-drawings there is found written by the pater-magister—"Done by Joshua out of pure idleness."   At a very early age "the Jesuit's Perspective" fell into his hands, and he studied it with such success that he was able to draw a correct representation of the colonnade beneath the school-house.   His first attempt in oil colours was made with a ship-painter's tools and colours in a boat-house, in company with a certain Dick Edgecumbe, of whom we hear more in the course of the narrative.

Jonathan Richardson was born in 1665, and died in 1745.   He was a portrait painter, though not of the highest class.   But he is best remembered by " An Essay on the whole Art of Criticism as it relates to Painting," and " An Argument in behalf of the Science of a Connoisseur."   One or both of these works—which Mr. Wornum says ought to be in every art library

—young Reynolds read, and they, he was wont
to say, " made him a painter." We cannot accept
Reynolds's definition of art-genius as being " great
general powers accidentally determined in a
particular direction," but such glowing and simple
enthusiasm as breathes in the words of Richardson were enough to raise the latent spark of
genius into a flame. Thenceforth his bias was
made manifest, and the " particular direction"
chosen. His father had some views of making
him a physician; but seeing his strong bent for
painting, he offered no resistance, and with entire
sympathy did what he could to forward his tastes
and interests. The pupil and son-in-law of
Richardson, Hudson, one of the Sir Godfrey school
of painters, was then at the head of the British
likeness-takers, prosperous and popular, and
Joshua was, at the age of seventeen, apprenticed
to him. The required fee was £120. Of this
one-half was borrowed from his sister, Mrs.
Palmer.

Hudson's pictures were dull, heavy, and formal.
The interest of the work was distributed with
great impartiality over the cocked hat, the ruffles,
the broad-sleeved coat, the waistcoat, and the
face. While standing *before* pictures of that

school the face cannot well be overlooked, but
when away from them the face cannot easily be
recalled to memory.  We endeavour to remember
it, but the broad-sleeved coat, the waistcoat, the
ruffles, and the cocked hat, that wearisome black
triangle usually being carried under the arm, are
too much for us.  We have to meditate on "the
fitness of things" before we are very sure that
there *was* a face.  And yet, strange to say, the
face was not so badly painted.  While the conception and relations of such pictures are de-
pressing, the execution is often good.  It is a
long road which the uneducated young artist has
to pass before he can mix oil-colours, and set eye,
nose, lip, in its place as well as Hudson did; and no
doubt young Reynolds, who had all the grammar
of his art to learn, looked with deep respect
on the pictures, finished and unfinished, which
hung round the studio of his new master, and
felt the dignity and responsibility of his position
when brought into the contact of even a subordinate with the great Sir Robert Walpole,
when that statesman came to have his velvet-
and-lace coat, his waistcoat, his wig, and his face
recorded with an equal, inanimate propriety.

Very slight records exist of the work done and

the life lived in Hudson's studio. Reynolds copied
the drawings of Guercino with great success, as
well as his master's pictures, and probably painted
in subordinate parts of the originals. So far as
the art of drawing and painting faces is concerned,
his opportunities were favourable enough. Beyond this they were barren in the extreme. The
young students of our own day can go to the
British Museum, the schools at South Kensington,
the schools of the Royal Academy, and find
plenty of casts from the antique to awaken effort,
to cultivate the sense of beauty, and to give
knowledge of the structure of the human figure,
and the requirements of pure outline. Few such
things would ever meet the eye of the pupil of
Hudson.

It will help us to look with tolerance on the
want of substantial knowledge of form, in all but
the head, from which Reynolds suffered through
life, if we reflect that—from the age of seventeen
to twenty, the years when the eye and memory
are most keen and strongly alive to impression—
he missed entirely that glorious instruction which
even the sight of the antique furnishes; and, consequently, that knowledge, the required extent of
which is not appreciated by less general observers,

but which Barry compares to enlarged geograph-
ical science. The promontories, hills, and vales of
the human face are difficult enough to map out, to
say nothing of their relation to expression ; but the
endless involutions of a human body, in its vary-
ing proportions between the Hercules and the
Venus—in its strange changes of contour under
muscular action, and especially in that refined
superficies of form and colour which overlays the
deep life below—constitute materials for a science
needing the best years of life for its acquirement.
Michael Angelo gained it in perfection ; but we
are told that he spent twelve years in the close
study of anatomy as one of the preliminaries of
its attainment. Twelve, twenty, or fifty years,
however, without the higher perception of the
relation of form to expression and action, would
be insufficient.

The wonder is that Reynolds, with such slender
opportunities, did so well ; nor is it reverent or
just for the youthful student, surrounded by
"Gladiators" and "Discoboli" from his school-
days, to affect contempt for the "drawing" of the
great master, who, till he was eight-and-twenty,
probably only knew the antique from bad prints,
or from a few maimed and yellow marbles,

brought over on "the grand tour" by *dilettanti*
noblemen. His study of the face must have been
profound; and the broad, deep, tender strength
with which from an early age he laid in the
features in their relative places, with their due
retiring subordination, shows how much he gained
by being shut up to a narrow circle of observation and study. There is a penalty often to be
paid for extended opportunities. Lawrence could
draw with immense knowledge and subtle grace;
but in his excess of science, we see, perhaps, one
of the causes of his inferiority to Reynolds in
painting the face. He knew too much for his
general powers. Reynolds's general powers always
exceeded his knowledge. A fine head by Reynolds
gives the impression of its having been painted by
a philosopher, which cannot be said of most works
from the more perturbed, if more scientific, pencil
of Sir Thomas Lawrence.

It is said that Reynolds left Hudson's studio
through some mutual misunderstanding. He remained, however, in after life in friendly relations with his old master; and though some slight
"tiff" might be the occasion of their parting, the
true reason probably was, that having seen how
to set the palette and paint the head throughout,

from dead colouring to glazing, and longing to
infuse life on his own account into heads tolerably
well painted, he began to tire of the everlasting
round of blue velvet and cocked hat.

Whether he made much way in society during
this early London sojourn, we are not informed.
He probably, at that time, saw and admired Garrick when he brought his quick and vivid powers
to bear on the dull and stilted forms of theatrical
art. An interesting anecdote of the period must
not be omitted. At a public auction, where
young Reynolds was present, there arose a buzz
and a whisper as the distorted form of the poet
Pope walked through a yielding crowd, dispensing
salutations and shaking hands, and not refusing
the hand of the youthful painter, stretched out in
an impulse of respectful enthusiasm. This, to
readers familiar with the incidents of the life of
Reynolds, is sure to recall a similar act of homage
paid by Northcote to Sir Joshua, on one of his
visits to Devonshire. Northcote touched the skirt
of his coat " with much satisfaction," delighted to
be so near the man whom he adored as a painter.

In the days when Daguerre was not, an
average skill in portraiture was a sure foundation
for respectable livelihood, if coupled with moderate

diligence, prudence, and manners. Reynolds became for a while a country artist. A delightful
little volume of sketches of country artists might
be written, after the manner of the shorter lives
of Allan Cunningham.

Till about the year 1855 there was no mode
of livelihood more secure and pleasant than that
of the unambitious country portrait painter of
any ability or conduct. Oil pictures of the heads
of households were things as necessary to equip-
ment as the sideboard and the sofa. The great
blemish on the mass of the tribe who supplied
this inevitable· demand was, perhaps, an excess of
conviviality.[1] Nothing placed two men, who had
dealings with each other in those days, on a more
pleasant footing than that of painter and sitter.
The sitter was desirous of looking his best in the
eyes of the painter, and of giving the best possible
impression of his person and character. He was
all smiles, all hospitality and concession. The
painter wished to see his subject at his ease. It
was seldom that the painter had not some other
unwonted gift. He sang or fiddled, or was a

[1] One of these men (who painted in the Sir William Beechey
style, red curtain and ruddy face), when asked at what period
of the day he painted best, replied, "I always paint *boldest*
after dinner."

mimic, or had "a fund of anecdote." His continual and varied intercourse with others gave
a charm to his manners, and he became the lion
of many a little country circle; but in much
danger, if he were not a man of higher tastes, of
sinking gradually into the red-nosed lodger at an
inn—the hero of a "portrait club"; the painter
of signs to clear off scores, and too often sinking
under a huge wave of work paid for, but unfinished, accumulated debts, and irresistible habits
of intemperance.

Reynolds, judging from his own account of
about three years of his young manhood, was in
some danger of declining into the free-and-easy
habits of his sect. He always lamented his waste
of time and opportunity at this period. After
the death of his father, in 1746, he took a house
at Plymouth Dock, and there lived with his two
unmarried sisters till 1749. Some attempts at
landscape, belonging to these years, are extant.
It was at about this period that he came into
contact with another and very important portion
of his teaching, the pictures of William Gandy,
of Exeter, whose father was a pupil of Vandyke.
Solemnity, force, and richness are said to mark
many of these pictures; and a traditional saying

of Gandy's, to the effect that the texture of oil paintings should resemble that of cream or cheese, weighed on the mind of Reynolds, and influenced him throughout his whole career. If the unlearned reader will look closely into the little picture of "Innocence" in the Vernon Gallery, he will understand what this technical aphorism meant.

It is interesting to observe, so far as prints can give the information, that Reynolds did not take any violent leap out of the Hudsonian position into his own higher walk. He moved upward on safe ground, and in his early portraits we can trace the process of animation and adventure. The shadows deepen, and the lights brighten here and there. The titled dame pushes her stiff shoulder a little further towards action, and sometimes ventures to lay her bent wrist on the waist, angling the elbow with spirit. The light veil begins to flutter; a stray lock is lifted by the breeze. "The dumb dead air," so particularly oppressive in the Hudson portrait, begins to roll and stir, and in due time we have the artist looking at us with an assured inquisitiveness from under his shading hand in the fine portrait which has been placed for us in the

National Portrait Gallery. He was early taken
under the patronage of Lord Edgecumbe, and it
was at Lord Edgecumbe's house that he met with
Commodore Keppel, to whose good offices thus
early in life so much of Reynolds's bright fortune
is owing. Both were young: Keppel, twenty-
four; Reynolds, twenty-six. *The Centurion* lay
in the Channel, bound for the coast of Africa.
Keppel generously offered to show his young
acquaintance something of the world and to take
him to Italy; thus a warm friendship commenced
which lasted through life, and was at all periods
of great professional advantage to the painter.
It also helped, undoubtedly, to give that political
complexion to his life which Mr. Taylor has
pointed out as being so significant.

Life on board a man-of-war for four months,
at that stage of a young artist's life, must have
been an important fact in his training, and the
character of Keppel must have influenced his
own. Keppel was of Dutch extraction, well born,
and valuing more than many (so says Burke)
the advantages of birth; yet he was frank,
friendly, and brave. In the Commodore's company he spent a week at Lisbon; saw the great
procession and the great bull-fight; saw Cadiz,

Gibraltar, Tetuan, Algiers, and at Algiers saw the Dey of Algiers, and witnessed a remarkable interview between that potentate and the bold and calm British officer, when that "beardless boy," as the Dey called him, threatened bombardment. At Minorca, the name of which was in a few years to become the keynote of popular fury, he was entertained so long that he had time to paint almost all the officers of the garrison. He asked but small prices, three guineas a head ; and to the rapid production of pictures at this price must be attributed something of the speed and facility for which his pencil was afterwards remarkable. It was at Minorca that he was thrown from his horse, and received that cut on the lip which gives so peculiar a cast to the Reynolds' mouth. In course of time he was landed at Leghorn, and entered the region of enchantment to all artists. He was now to see what Richardson had taught him to wonder at, and almost to worship. He hastened onwards to Rome, and another and the most important stage of his education began.

It is a soothing prelude to the marvellously active life of Reynolds, to hear his account of the manner in which those two years were spent in

Rome. There is an expression occurring more than once in these memoirs, that shows his development to have been, though cautious and slow at first, by no means accidental. "I considered," says he, "that I had *a great game to play.*" He sat down to his great game with eminent deliberation. That he might have time for study, he borrowed money from his married sisters, who seem to have been in good circumstances. He did not seek commissions from the travelling lords who were willing to pay for copies of notable works. He did not copy, during all his stay in Italy, more than a very few of the great pictures. He did not paint serious portraits. He did, though, what is exceedingly anomalous. He painted two or three of that uninteresting class of pictures, called in those days "*caricaturas.*" One of these, representing some noisy funny scene between tutor, lord, courier, and innkeeper, was exhibited not long ago at the British Institution, and showed but a feeble sense of humour, with not much painting power. It had the look of work done to oblige a patron who mistook, as men often do, verbal or historic humour for pictorial. His method was to make small studies and sketches, according to their

relation to the governing excellence of the work
before him, and plenty of written memoranda
and slight pencillings for the purpose of fixing on
his memory the great things he might never, and
as it proved did never, see again.

The years 1750 and 1751 were passed in this
way to memorable advantage, and under very
favourable conditions. It is pleasant to imagine
him during this happy recess, sitting, standing, or
lying, "through whole solemn hours," under the
awful shades of the Sistine, "capable of the emo-
tions which Michael Angelo intended to excite,"
or waiting breathless with close investigation
before the "Heliodorus," or the "Miracle of
Bolsena," or the "Disputa," or that airy Hill of
the Muses, till the true light of taste dawned
upon him, and he felt himself able to understand
what, he confesses with genuine simplicity, he was
at first sight unable thoroughly to receive or
enjoy. By the way, this would be a good subject
for a note to another edition of the *Modern
Painters*,—"How far was Reynolds right in his
first impression of Raphael, and wrong in his
second?" Mr. Ruskin's analysis of the cartoon
of "Christ's Charge to Peter," in the third volume
of *Modern Painters*, may be compared with

Reynolds's first and instinctive judgment of the pictures in the Vatican.

After Rome he visited Florence, Bologna, and Venice, conceiving too high an opinion of the eclectic schools, but finding what he was best fitted to understand and love in Venice among the works of Titian, Veronese, the Bassani, and Tintoretto.

In 1752, on the 16th of October, Reynolds arrived in London, and laid down the first stake in the great game he proposed to play.

His capital consisted of a body and mind charged to the full with life, health, energy—the grammar of Hudson, the hints of Gandy, the rapid practice of Plymouth and Minorca, the "grand gusto" of Rome, the combinations of Bologna, and the superb ornamentalism of Venice, the experience of a traveller, the rudiments of a scholar, and the capacity of a philosopher. In addition, he had made some mechanical preparations; he had contrived that some prelusive strains of fame should reach the ears of London before he arrived, and he brought with him an Italian " drapery man."

The drapery man was a necessary appendage in every fashionable studio of those days. Unless

a little of the manufactory is conjoined with the
higher uses of art, fortune cannot be secured, and
to our minds it is very observable that position,
taken in the social sense, and fortune in the
banking sense, were distinct and important parts
of the great Reynolds's "game." *He meant to have
everything the earth could give him, and he got it.*
The name of the young Italian was Giuseppe
Marchi, and one of his master's earliest doings
was a portrait of his pupil in a turban. It is not
an astounding picture; and Hudson told him
plainly that he did not paint so well as before he
went to Italy.

Reynolds did not return to a soil entirely
barren of art, though it was barren of all patronage
except for portrait painting. In 1750 Hogarth's
"Marriage à la Mode" was knocked down at a
public auction for £110. The frames alone of
this series cost him £24, so that for these match-
less works he was paid at the rate of less than
£15 each. He had shown great ability in
portraiture long before this. The portrait of
Captain Coram, at the Foundling Hospital, is full
of life and power, as no doubt was many another
from the same hand. He was not fitted, however, either by his skill or manners, to take the

place of a popular portrait painter. At this time
he had mistaken his way, and was at work on
sacred subjects. He had the " Paul before Felix "
on his easel. If Paul had been what his accusers
said he was, " a pestilent fellow," and Felix a
Bow Street magistrate, Hogarth was the man to
have given us an immortal work—the real Paul
and Felix were above his reach.

Richard Wilson had been a portrait painter,
but was now beginning that sorrowful career of
landscape—landscape poetic, forlorn and grand—
which helped so much to raise our landscape art,
and so little to supply his own necessities. A
Swiss painter, Liotard, was in possession of the
field of portrait just then. He was a *neat* painter,
but his neatness could not stand long before the
importation of novelty, life, and strength fresh
from abroad, and he disappeared.

The first work of Reynolds which attracted
public attention was a vigorous full length of
Commodore Keppel, standing on a stormy sea-
shore, and with animation giving directions to
unseen figures on the beach. The attitude was
adapted from a pencil sketch of an antique
statue picked up somewhere in his travels,
and marks from the first his habit of using

the ideas of others whenever he could do so
with advantage.

Leslie, in his charming *Handbook for Young
Painters*, has a remark which will help us to
estimate Reynolds all the more accurately. "I
have no hesitation," he writes, "in saying, that
every artist whose name has lived, owes his immortality more to the excellence of his taste, than
to any other single endowment; because it displays
all the rest to their fullest advantage, and without
it his mind would be imperfectly seen; and if
taste be not the highest gift of the painter, it is,
I think, the rarest." This rare gift was possessed
by Reynolds in an unwonted degree. This and
another characteristic, midway between taste and
humour—the power to see "the weak side of
things"—enabled him to use the inventions of
others with consummate judgment. His fine eye
and delicate hand, so cool and light, enabled him
to give the charm of freshness and naturalness,
which prevented the spectator from tracing the
origin of his ideas. His mind was appreciative,
not inventive. He saw no visions; he dreamed
no dreams. But he was alive to the airiest and
most subtle charms of the visible. All in his life
and thinking was eminently actual and outward.

It is where the mind is equally balanced between the visionary spontaneity of imagination, and the quiet, keen perception of outward fact, that the few highest masters of art are manifested,—the Michael Angelo, the Raphael, the Titian, the Shakespeare,—and no man of this class can consent to borrow, though occasionally, as Raphael did, he may condescend to adapt.

His first house was at No. 104 St. Martin's Lane, near the studio of Roubiliac. He removed soon after to No. 5 Great Newport. Street, his sister Frances taking the management of his house. The brother and sister were not congenial souls. He was even ; she was fretful and full of "megrims." She painted miniatures, and copied her brother's pictures. "These copies," said her brother, "make other people laugh and me cry." After a few years they separated. The principles on which he commenced his life-work are early apparent, and continued ever after to guide him. He had a settled, and indeed an exaggerated, conviction of the importance of labour. Feeling his slowness of invention, he made the best reflection under the circumstances—namely, that great facility often induces haste and carelessness. The tortoise in the actual result of the race of

life not seldom distances the hare. He began
with the determination to "go to his studio
willing or unwilling, morning, noon, and night,"
a resolve differing from that of Stothard, who
walked the streets daily for hours, drinking in
health, and catching sudden and fleeting graces
from the moving life around him.  Reynolds was
too much of an indoor artist all his life.  He
took, however, every pains to learn painting from
paintings.  He bought what good works of the
old masters he could afford to buy; he "even
borrowed money for that purpose, believing them
to be for a painter the best kind of wealth."  He
went so far as to tell Northcote, that "for a
really fine specimen of Titian he would consent
to ruin himself."  He died worth eighty thousand
pounds in money, and surely if he had only *half*
ruined himself, he might have attained his wish.
He thought India-stock valuable as well as
Titians, and tried to dispose of his Titians before
he died.

He made systematic experiments in effect and
colour, "leaving out every colour in turn, and
showing it that he could do without it."  He
peered into, and chipped, and filed away and
dissolved portions of old paintings to get at the

"Venetian secret." In painting his pictures he exhibited, perhaps, his most marked peculiarity of mind, always looking on them "as a whole." It is this breadth of view, this tendency to generalise and mass, this breath of the philosophic spirit, which gives so much of the air of greatness to his works.

At first his use of materials was tolerably simple and safe. The aim at brilliance and richness induced him from the first to use fleeting colours if they were splendid in hue. It may be questioned whether he was not misled afterwards by the Gandy theory about cream and cheese. In his more successful efforts after this quality there is a species of charm on close inspection. But not only is it true that at the focal distance mere richness of pigment is lost, but it may also be respectfully denied that human flesh is like "cream or cheese" in texture. It is not like anything which may not be successfully imitated with such simple media as Gainsborough used. There is a tendency in some artists and connoisseurs to confuse the sweetness of the face with the sweetness of something to eat, and to such eyes the dry and airy world is "embedded and enjellied" in unctuous semi - transparency.

D

One of the cant phrases of this school goes beyond the Gandy idea. It is accounted to be an
excellence in a picture that it should look
" buttery."

We meet with one excellent resolve in the
beginning of his public life, the want of which
spoils many a young painter,—to do his best at
each succeeding picture whether the subject were
attractive or not. Moreover, his "grand tour,"
his Italian studies, his many qualifications, did
not overwhelm his prudence. He began to paint
at the very moderate price of five guineas a
head.

The political sketches which fill so many
pages of the book, interesting and well written as
they are, may be passed lightly over; for, except
that Reynolds's career was undoubtedly influenced
by his early associations with the party in opposition, we meet with no expressions of political
sentiment, and only one political act,—his voting
for Fox,—and we have abundant evidence that to
him a man's politics were no barrier to intercourse. He was found one day at the table of
Wilkes, and the next day he dined with Johnson;
and, during the grand and celebrated "Impeach-
ment," we find him on one day sharing the

hospitality of Warren Hastings, and the next he
has his feet under the table of Burke.

The times of his appearance before the world
are not pleasant to read of.  " Coarse, rollicking,
and hearty " they were; drinking and gambling,
and dissolute times in a degree that disgusts,
while the narrative of it amuses; days of fearful
political corruption, when men would do anything
for power, when the Paymaster of the Forces
thought it no shame to pocket the interest of
the money in his hands, and when "secret service
money" meant money for buying votes for the
Government.  Truly, " the canker of peace " looked
festering enough, and there is a sort of pleasure
in seeing the wild passion of the upper-class
men of those days becoming purged and noble
with the bursting out of " the blossom of war
with a heart of fire."  It seems better that they
should die bravely among the thunders of the
fleet in Newfoundland mists, or leave their bones
in the parched Carnatic, than thrust one another
through in the stews of London.

Into the mixed society of this era Reynolds
was well prepared to enter.  He had, young as
he was, seen much good company.  He had firm
nerves, a quiet unobtrusive self-reliance, and his

speech was considerate and wise. He had none
of that moodiness and inequality of temper so
often the counterbalance of genius; yet, as we
see by many instances, there was, under a calm
exterior, a spirit of insatiable curiosity and restless observation. Little disturbed by thronging
fancies from within, he was free to fix with more
accuracy on impressions from without, and gather
them home there for his use. People who had
no great public events to fill mouths were talking
of *Sir Charles Grandison*, Gray's *Elegy*, *Peregrine
Pickle*, and Johnson's Dictionary, and it was not
long before he crossed the path of *Ursa Major*
himself. They were friends at a stroke. They
first met at the house of the daughters of Admiral
Cotterell. One of the ladies lamented the death
of a friend to whom they were under great obliga-
tions. "You will," said the penetrating young
portrait painter, who had seen the world out of
the studio as well as in it, "at least be set free
from the burden of obligation." This acute,
caustic, and daring saying caught the quick ear
of Johnson. It was "of a higher mood" than
the commonplaces of polite society. He went
home to sup with Reynolds, and in this way
commenced a long friendship, founded in mutual

esteem and admiration, between two men as dissimilar in most respects as could well be.  Their
acquaintance was a fortunate occurrence for both.
In Johnson, Reynolds found his most influential
teacher; and in Reynolds, Johnson found his
tenderest and most considerate friend.

As yet, the star of Burke, who was to rise,
according to Macaulay, "in amplitude of com-
prehension and richness of imagination superior
to every orator ancient or modern," was below
the horizon.  He was then twenty-three years
old, reading for the bar, contributing to papers
and periodicals, turning over in his mind the
question of the propriety of his emigrating, or the
prospect of a consulship, and meditating on "the
sublime and beautiful."  Goldsmith, at the age
of twenty-five, was going northward to study
medicine, to learn, as Beauclerk put it afterwards,
"to kill those who were not his enemies."  Reynolds himself was nearly thirty, well trained, and
in the best order for the race of life.

In 1754 there was a great awakening of public
interest and excitement.  The horizons east and
west, in India and America, were troubled, and,
says Reynolds's biographer, "few periods of our
history were more stirring than the years from

1754 to 1760." To any one interested at once in history and in art, the connection between the public events of the whole period of Reynolds's activity and the shadowy studio in which so many of the remarkable men of the time sat from year to year, would be an exceedingly delightful branch of study, and would help to realise and enkindle his conception of the time. So many engravings exist from the long series of Reynolds's portraits, that a very complete historic collection may be hung in the galleries of the mind from this source alone; and this is, of course, the thread of connection by which the historic and biographic portions of the *Life* under consideration is bound together. In 1755 we find the painter in fully established business, and are able, from this date, to follow his doings pretty closely by means of those pocket-books which it would be a pleasure to see and handle; filled slowly from day to day, through a course of nearly forty years, with names that create a slight thrill as we read them, and rendered the more racy from a certain want of genius for spelling, which was a small set-off against so many other excellent gifts.

In this first recorded year we have not less than 120 sitters. Two portraits per week (when

many of them would be large and some full-
length pictures) seems hard work ; but we must
remember the valuable co-operation of "the
drapery man." It was a point with him never to
be seen out of his studio in the daytime ; perhaps, for him, with his indoors' imagination, the
best course. But it would seem as if he were
equally careful, except when he received company,
never to be found at home after dark. He lived
in the age of clubs. He made the club his library
and news-room, and had the good sense to choose
as companions those who could teach him ; men
whose business it was to read, think, and write.
His close study was of pictures ; but he was a
shrewd, humorous, and delighted observer of life
and manners. He was not a talker, and hated
talking artists, but he was a delicate, discrimina-
tive, and generous *listener*. The ear-trumpet is
typical. In his power of listening with intelli-
gence lies one of the great secrets of his power of
making and keeping such dissimilar friends as
Johnson, Burke, Goldsmith, Gibbon, Wilkes, and
a host of others, who, at constant feud with each
other, were all agreed in their warm attachment
to Reynolds.

He began with an artists' club, and at

"Slaughter's Coffee House" met weekly with his old master, Hudson, with Roubiliac, the sculptor, Gravelot and M'Ardell, the engravers, Hogarth and Frank Hayman, rough and ready. We have now to trace broadly a career of unexampled good fortune, reaching over two-and-twenty years, in which no rival showed his face, and during which he was the lord paramount of portraiture in Britain. Of the 120 names of sitters recorded in the first pocket-book, a fourth are those of people of high title, beside two or three admirals, as many baronets, colonels, and captains. Among the admirals are Lord Anson, then resting from his labours in the dignity of First Lord of the Admiralty, and Boscawen, painted immediately before he set sail for Newfoundland on the breaking out of hostilities with France. There is the name of Lord Ligonier, a French Protestant refugee, who became Generalissimo, one of Marlborough's heroes. He died in 1770, at the age of ninety-two. It is supposed that Reynolds's endeavour to paint the old man's features as they might have appeared years before in the fields of Flanders, led to its being, as it certainly is, poorly painted as to the face. For seven laborious years Reynolds seems to have thrown all his powers

into the work of achieving a position. He
worked incessantly, and with rapidly developing
power. The portrait of Dr. Johnson, which was
engraved in Boswell's *Life*, where he is sitting
in a homely, check-covered chair, by a homely
table, into which he is plunging his left fist, or
dropping it like a paw, the legs wide apart, the
head hung heavily aside, the eyes looking askance
for his weighty idea which the charged pen waits
to record, was done in 1756, and shows how
much life and daring his pencil had by this time
acquired.

During that heaving and convulsive year, when
war blazed out all over the world, he seems to
have worked harder than at any period of his
career. Northcote remarks the year 1758 as
having been the busiest of all Reynolds's years.
He painted in it the surprising number of 150
portraits. William of Culloden, now less favour-
ably known as William of Kloster Seven, is found
among this mass of subjects; Lady Coventry, one
of the celebrated Miss Gunnings of the year when
he returned from Italy, and now dying of consumption; Commodore Edgecumbe, "fresh from
the triumphs of Louisbourg"; and Mrs. Horneck,
hereafter to be better known as the friend of

Goldsmith—have their names on this year's list; and as showing the martial spirit of the time, and an admirable type of it, the striking full length of Sir Francis Deleval as a volunteer, evidently defying the world, by all that is signified between musket-stock and bayonet-point, his hat cocked bravely on his head.

Mrs. Pelham, feeding her chickens, abundantly more charming than if she were sacrificing to the Graces, or wielding the bow of Diana with a three-inch crescent perched on her head-dress, also sat or stood; and the extravagant and lively Kitty Fisher, so often afterwards painted by Reynolds, now represented as nursing doves, with a dove-like grace and innocence of look, but belonging to a class of which the dove is not the most appropriate emblem. Many of this class were brought to him from time to time, La Renas and Checcinas, Phrynes and Thaises, whom he painted for the random gambling lords who imported them. Kitty Fisher is said to have squandered £12,000 in nine months. It was this Cleopatra-like profusion which probably suggested to Reynolds the not unapt rendering of her in the character of the "swarthy queen with bold black eyes," dissolving a pearl in her wine cup.

Seamen lately renowned for gallant actions
with French privateers were there ; admirals who
saw Wolfe land at Quebec, and brought home the
news of his death ; soldiers came to tell how the
day went on the field of Minden, or left his studio
to fall amid the smoke of Kempen, or to mix in
other onsets in that dreadful, useless struggle for
the province of Silesia, " for the sake of which the
life-blood of more than a million was poured out
like water." " Yellow Jacks " and " Black Dicks,"
dogged commodores and daring captains ; Lord
George Sackville and the Colonel Fitzroy who
took the disobeyed orders of Prince Ferdinand to
Lord George on the field ; commanders of secret
expeditions ; colonels who had stood round George
the Second in battle, and one (Colonel Trapaud)
who prevented the king's horse from rushing into
the French lines ; are all found in turn seated in
the quiet studio chair, with their stories of march
and charge and beleaguerment by the Rhine, the
Weser, or the Elbe.

Country mayors, like Sir William Blackett,
whose picture is in the Infirmary at Newcastle-
on-Tyne ; clerical men and men of learning, such
as Dr. Markham, afterwards Archbishop of York ;
comedians like Harry Woodward, " brisk and

breezy"; tragedians like Barry, and one who lived
between both comedy and tragedy like Garrick;
are succeeded by men

> Wearing a lofty and a serious brow,
> Sad, high, and working full of state and woe,

like Sir Septimus Robinson, Usher of the Black
Rod, whose sittings are "always very early"; and
mixed with these "a bevy of fair women richly
dressed"; duchess, and marchioness, and countess,
and lady; the noble's mistress; the squire's dame
and young ones, the father's pride and the mother's
joy.   Such a bringing together of the image of an
age as is only seen in the studio of the fashionable
portrait painter.

One of the very memorable portraits of this
stage of Reynolds's career is that of Laurence
Sterne, the lion of society, whom to meet, "it was
needful," says Gray the poet, "to have invitations
a fortnight beforehand."   On this picture Leslie
makes the subtle criticism that he is not simply
resting his head on his hand as in thought, but is
at the same time propping himself up, as one in
feeble health, and that the wig is tilted slightly on
the head, giving it the rakish Shandean air which
characterises it.   The whole picture is individual;
the eyes stare and burn impudently close under

the square brow ; the expression, so incongruous
with a clerical costume, is that of one who neither
fears God nor regards man.  This picture was presented to Sterne by Reynolds, and might possibly
be a repayment of the most compact and felicit-
ous description of the style of Reynolds which .
we know.  " Reynolds himself, *great and graceful
as he paints,* might have painted him as he sat."
Sterne tampered with the pencil on his own account, and would know how to value such a gift.
The resolute diligence and freedom from all rivalry
of these first seven years; the increase of his prices,
which had gradually risen from five to twenty-five
guineas, while the full length had reached a hundred guineas, had so enlarged his means as to
warrant his removal to a larger house at No. 47
Leicester Square.  He gave £1650 for a forty
years' lease (which he almost lived to see expired),
made additions to the extent of £1500 more, in
the shape of a gallery and studio, and at the early
age of thirty-seven set up his carriage—a gorgeous
affair indeed—painted as to the panels with the
four seasons by Catton, and furnished with foot-
men in silver lace.  This outburst exhausted his
savings ; but, as his practice was large and his
diligence great, he was able soon to replenish his

purse, and to lay the foundation of an ample
fortune.  We find that ere long his yearly income
amounted to £6000.

Here, already remarkable for the snuff (Hard-
man's, 37 Strand) and the ear-trumpet which
single him out to the eye, he was found established
at the accession of George the Third.

The Royal Marriage took place in 1761, and
one of the best of his allegorical pictures was soon
after painted,—that of Lady Elizabeth Keppel, one
of the bridesmaids, sister of his early friend the
Commodore.  She was represented in the character
of a votary adorning the altar of Hymen with long
wreaths of flowers, and attended by a maiden who
is preparing some sort of libation in an urn.  The
huge Earl of Errol sat about the same time, "a
colossus in cloth of gold," whom Horace Walpole
compared to "one of the giants in the Guildhall
new-gilt."

The spirits sink unaccountably among these
allegorical pictures in spite of the classics and the
gods.  Among his Didos embracing Cupid, his
Hopes and Loves and Graces, it is pleasing to
come upon the natural and probable group of
Lady Sarah Lennox and Lady Susan Strangways,
with the youthful Charles James Fox.  One of

the ladies leans out of window, the other raises a
dove to her caress, and the young Fox invites them
to a rehearsal. The red bricks of Holland House
look more real and stimulating than the gloomy
mausoleums and prophetic cells in which his
unvowed "votaries" are performing their sham
sacrifices that make us yawn vehemently and
wish they were over. The Earl of Bute in blue
velvet and gold, the Princess Augusta, the witty,
careless, clever, unprincipled Charles Townshend,
the proposer of that memorable Colonial Stamp
Act which set a-ringing the ominous muffled bells
of Boston (and who made the wicked joke on
another sitter, a stout and wealthy heiress, that
"her tonnage was equal to her poundage"). Lord
Holland; Lord Chief-Justice Pratt, afterwards Lord
Camden, and closely concerned in the after dis-
putes as to the legality of general warrants; Lord
Granby, Master-General of Ordnance, and the
subject of one of his most striking whole lengths;
Count Lippe Schaumburg, "soldier, statesman, and
man of letters,"—found their way early to the new
studio in Leicester Square. The Count's picture
is a large full length on a square canvas. He
stands, long-faced, long-chinned, dark-eyed, at
once pleasant and grim, against a wild sky full

of rolling glooms and gleams, and in the shade
around him finely disposed emblems of war —
mortar, and cannon-wheel, and ball, a charger
with ruffled mane below, a banner with dropping
fold behind him.   Equally fine is the Vandyke-
like portrait of Sir Geoffrey Amherst, in plate
armour, his helmet resting on some plan of siege
or battlefield.

Hogarth died in 1764, and the Literary Club
was formed the same year, meeting till 1775 at
the Turk's Head in Gerrard Street.   During the
summer the ceaseless and ardent toils of Reynolds
told upon his health, and he was laid aside for a
while by severe illness.   All that relates to that
glorious circle, gathered round "the brown table"
at "the Club," is intensely attractive.   It was the
intellectual centre of the time.   There Johnson
ruled, "predominating" like the huge bear over
the gate of the Baron of Bradwardine.   Our feelings veer like the wind as we look at the bulk and
texture of the "literary leviathan," so strangely
put together.   At one moment the eye moistens
in admiration of his nobility and tenderness ; at
another moment we shrink and collapse as if we
had been personally struck down and trampled in
unexpected assault.

We see Edmund Burke, who raises our conceptions of the possibilities of human nature, and
touches us, like the prelude of an oratorio, with
the sense of wonder and expectancy. Burke was
a match for Johnson in talk. Reynolds was his
match also, but in another way, and the Doctor .
found and pronounced him "invulnerable." A
constant association with every class of men and
women; a quick, quiet eye, which could discover
the coming storm at a distance; a genial and not
easily ruffled temper (to the excellence of which,
the most striking if somewhat strongly pronounced
testimony is that of Northcote, that "you might
put the *Divil* on Reynolds's back, without putting
him in a fidget"); a perception of "the weak side
of things," which Goldsmith lacked; and a well-
filled purse, carried Reynolds through thirty years
of close association with Dr. Johnson with scarcely
a ripple of discordance, and it confirms our admiration of the firmness and expansiveness of Reynolds's understanding, that he should cultivate so
near an intercourse with one who, beside being
purblind, or, perhaps, partly because he *was* purblind, had not the least sympathy with the
painter's pursuits. The Biography gives many
interesting and graphic notices of the doings

E

and sayings of this memorable club, and Mr.
Taylor has found such fascination in even its wine
accounts, that he gives us the average consumption
per man of the port and claret, which were the
main beverages.

Reynolds was one of the most regular attend-
ants there, but he by no means confined his attention to this awful centre of intellectual law. He
seems to have been as fond of the society of men
of fashion as men of literature and art. He was
a frequenter of a notorious club composed of
"maccaronis" and "bloods," whose chief pursuits
were hard drinking, deep gaming, and blasphemous profanity. Here he was distinguished for his
ceremonious politeness and his bad whist-playing.
Through all his laborious life we see in him
nothing of the dreamy, secluded student. When
not at his easel he was about among men; beef-
steak clubs, *sçavoir vivre* clubs, *saur-kraut* clubs,
ladies' clubs, gambling clubs; no clubs came amiss
to him where "life" was to be seen. Along with
clubs came endless dinner engagements, as various
as his portraits; great dukes and lords, bishops
and politicians, Wilkes and Johnson, Burke and
Warren Hastings, keen-tongued, card-playing
Kitty Clive, all these, as well as, or more often

than, the artist or connoisseur, were his daily
table companions.    When dinners were over, then
to Vauxhall and Ranelagh, and the Pantheon
and Mrs. Corneley's masquerades, to balls and
assemblies, to "chaoses," and queer collections
of "blues."   While Gainsborough, in after years,
sat by his lamp at home throwing his exquisite
sketches under the table, or Romney, whose
"solitude was sublime," brooded in front of his
cartoons, Reynolds was still in and out of the
congregations of men.

It is this ceaseless energy, this tranquil vivacity, this unappeasable curiosity for the things of
the present, that formed a very large element and
a very central secret of his great power and influence.   He also knew the meaning of the saying
of Ulysses—

> To have done is to hang
> Quite out of fashion, like a rusty mail,
> In monumental mockery . . .
> For emulation hath a thousand sons,
> That one by one pursue ; if you give way,
> Or hedge aside from the direct forthright,
> Like to an entered tide, they all rush by
> And leave you hindmost.

To complete the image of exuberant life, we must
see him occasionally on horseback going across

country after the hounds, or in the stubble bag-
ging the game, or betting Mr. Parker five guineas
that he will hit a mark. Alive, alert, with next
to unfailing health and unflagging spirits, we see
him gathering more of the materials of a whole
success than any man of his time. It was not in
the supreme force of any one gift that we discern
the pre-eminence of our Sir Joshua. He aimed at
fame, and fortune, and influence, and the enjoyment of the passing hour, and at general culture
so far as it could be obtained by a thoroughgoing
man of the world, as he undoubtedly was. He
looked after the small things that enhance success.
In the poem written by Warton on the Oxford
Window, he is desirous to have his name "hitched
in," so that the praise may have its full personal
force ; and he made his sister ride about in his
gilded coach, that people might ask, if Northcote
does not mislead us, "Whose coach is that?" and
that people might answer, "That is the coach of
Sir Joshua Reynolds, the eminent portrait painter."

Perhaps the political event in which Reynolds
would be most likely to have a strong personal
interest was the brief accession to power of the
Rockingham administration, in which the Edmund
Burke of the club and the Edmund Burke of Rey-

nolds's counsels and affections was "the foremost
man." In an age when all good things were
bought and sold, the sight of "a ministry who
practised no corruption, nor were ever suspected
of any, sold no offices, obtained no reversions or
pensions, either coming in or going out, for themselves, their families, or their dependants," is
soothing and cheering, and sheds a pleasant reflected light on the course of this biography. The
splendour was soon eclipsed. In 1782 it gleamed
out again like the sun on an October day, but
we see the long course of Burke's magnificent life
passed in the shade and storm of opposition, to
die out under the lurid conflagration, which was
mistaken for sunrise, of the French Revolution.

In 1768 Reynolds paid a visit to Paris, setting
out on the 9th of September, with Richard Burke,
the talkative, light-hearted, and random brother
of Edmund. They had only two breaks-down in
their posting; saw Abbeville, Amiens, St. Just,
Chantilly, St. Denis, the galleries, the theatres,
Préville and Molé; "lay at Sittingbourne" on the
return journey; and arrived in London on the
8th of October.

On the 9th of December Reynolds was hailed
President of the Royal Academy, which had been

formed in his absence, and shortly afterwards he left a sitter for the *levée* and returned—Sir Joshua Reynolds—to his usual labours. These honours made Johnson break his resolution against wine, and we may fancy the scene at No. 47, when his health was drunk by Burke and the rest of that high company.

The scheme of an Academy of Arts was first originated in 1755, between the artists and the Dilettanti Society. It was placed on its present basis in this year of 1768. It has been frequently, sometimes violently attacked. Leslie here enters on an elaborate defence and eulogy of it. His *collaborateur* differs from him; and it is not unfair to refer to the expressed opinions of Mr. Taylor, seeing that they are accessible to all in a blue-book. Mr. Taylor was examined by the royal commission which sat to investigate the constitution of the Academy in 1863. He speaks mildly of the Academy in the Life of Reynolds; but not with much warm approval in the blue-book. The most real ground of assault has not been, however, against the Royal Academy *as* an academy. It is out of the annual exhibition over which it has the control that so many heart-burnings have chiefly arisen. There is no other arena

open to the artist where there is anything like a
fair opportunity of being seen by the generality of
buyers and patrons ; yet it has been thought that
the interests of members of the Academy have
been too exclusively consulted. They have a right
to send a large number of works year by year, and
to have these works hung in the best places. If
their works were necessarily more excellent than
others, this would not be felt to be a grievance.
In the early days of the institution its members
included every good painter. It is not so now ;
and seeing that there are and have been in recent
times so many painters of acknowledged power
and genius not numbered amongst the members
of the Academy, no young painter of ability will
be, for the honour's sake, very anxious to add the
mystic letters to his name. Still, there is the
question of the market. If work is not seen it
cannot be bought, and where can it be efficiently
seen by the mass of buyers but at the Royal
Academy ?

To our mind the whole system of temporary
exhibition is unpleasant. The crush, the heat, the
whirl, the golden flames that blaze round the walls,
the mass of incongruous subjects huddled together,
unfit the very organs of vision for correct seeing,

and the mind for correct judging, and we dream
of something more adapted to the wants of both
painter and buyer: some long, quiet, accessible,
well-known galleries where, if need be the year
round, as the pictures hung at the National
Galleries, or in the corridors of South Kensington,
the newly-finished work may be put up and removed at pleasure, and where it may be seen
without distraction. At present all is bitter contest—contest for admission, contest for proper
hanging, contest for public applause. Now and
then on the walls of South Kensington, the young
painter's Paradise, we see a new picture (how it
came there we know not, for the place is like a
fairy palace, where unseen fingers work constantly
new wonders), such as G. F. Watts's "Sisters."
The delight of coming on such work with cool
nerves and unthrobbing eyes is extreme.

Concerning the relative value and placing of
the paintings in the exhibition of 1863, Mr.
Taylor says, "This year the worst pictures in
almost every department of art, represented in the
Royal Academy, are by Royal Academicians."
And again he says, in conclusion, "I doubt
whether the Royal Academy exercises an influence for good. The education is most defective,

and the exhibition is not such as it ought to be to
enhance the character of British art ; it popularises
it, but it does not raise it."

But whatever the Academy may be *now*, we
have reason to be thankful for what it has done
for art in this country.   It has called public
attention to art.   It consolidated and trained the
art spirit.   It gave us Stothard, and Turner, and
Wilkie, and Hilton, and Landseer, and Leslie.
And its first president and most splendid name
was Sir Joshua Reynolds.

He was now at the summit of fame and
influence.   He had taken a villa at Richmond,
and had joined the life there as in London.   He
appears at the Richmond Assembly, and Mr.
Taylor suggests that he very likely took lessons
of Noverre, the great dancing master of the day.

We find the club in 1768 anxious about Goldsmith's new comedy.   In the life of Johnson,
Oliver Goldsmith stands out for more than a
dozen years a conspicuous figure ; but under the
tempered light of the studio in Leicester Square,
we see him in a more favourable aspect, and one
more pleasant to our view.   He was not laughed
at, or cowed, or "knocked down with the butt end"
of an argument there.   Reynolds loved him, and

painted him with the utmost tenderness of thought.
Leslie has given us a fine criticism on this portrait,
to which it is worth the reader's while to turn.
Reynolds knew from experience that thought and
inward power may exist where the faculty of rapid
or collected utterance is denied to the tongue,—
and the man of whom Garrick said, that he "wrote
like an angel and talked like poor Poll," found a
shelter in the sympathy of the man he learned
to love like a brother.   In the dedication to Sir
Joshua of *The Deserted Village*, Goldsmith wrote :
"Setting interest aside, to which I never paid
much attention, I must be indulged at present in
following my affections.   The only dedication I
ever made was to my brother, because I loved
him better than most other men.   He is since
dead.   Permit me to inscribe this poem to you."

Johnson was subsisting at this time on sub-
scriptions to his Shakespeare, without the fortitude to record either the sums received or the
names sent in.   His friends were anxious about
his honour, and Reynolds offered to assist him
with his pen.   He helped him also with three
contributions to *The Idler*.

Reynolds found his pen a more serviceable
instrument than his tongue, and did his best to

train it.   He projected and delivered from time
to time a series of Discourses to the students of
the Royal Academy.   The first of these was given
on the 2nd of January 1769.   He was not an
orator.   His voice was indistinct, his delivery dry
and tame, but he was full of the sense of the intellectual importance of the art he professed.   He
congratulated the students that they had nothing
to unlearn, exhorted them to obey rules, to take
pains, and to remember that "nothing is denied
to well-directed labour," that "labour will improve
natural gifts," that "labour will even supply their
deficiency," which may be in matters of art abundantly questioned.

It is curious to read the innumerable little
episodes of his stirring life : such as his visits
to Wilkes when in hiding ;  his dinners with
him when in the King's Bench prison, and
the accounts of the changeful society with
which his evenings were spent.   But we must
hasten on.

It is to Northcote that we owe some of the
most intimate and trustworthy details of the life
of Reynolds.   He became a pupil in the house of
the painter, and left it after five years' faithful
service.   He was a man of third-rate ability in

the art, but he ardently loved it and most sincerely admired Reynolds. He talked to the end
of his days the broad Devonshire dialect which he
brought to Leicester Square, and which Reynolds
loved to hear. Under Hazlitt's pen in later years
he appears a querulous, caustic, sagacious, penurious old man, with hollow and wizard-like eyes.
In Leicester Square we see another figure—the
busy, faithful, listening, provincial assistant, for-
warding the huge full length, and astounded with
mingled vexation and admiration when Sir Joshua
enters, and with great strokes of the brush sweeps
away into effective generalisation the careful work
of days, or swoops on one of his pictures done from
the tame eagle in the back-yard, to make it a bird
of Jove by a few rufflings of the hand of the master.
"The Prince of Wales says he knows you; where
did you make his acquaintance?" asked Sir Joshua.
"The Prince of Wales does *not* know me," answered
Northcote; "it is only *his brag*."

In 1772 Reynolds painted Sir Joseph Banks,
then newly returned from the expedition to Ota-
heite for the purpose of observing the transit of
Venus. Here, again, the lively curiosity of his
nature is displayed. He sought as frequently as
he could the society of Banks and Solander, and

took the utmost interest in all their discoveries
and observations.

It was Reynolds's habit, when not employed
with portraits, to paint small fancy pictures, the
models for which he found for the most part
among the tribe of beggars—old men and children.  He had painted the study of a head from a
favourite high-featured old man, formerly a pavior,
by name George White, now reduced to beggary.
This picture was seen by Burke and others, and
pointed out as being an admirable suggestion for
the head of Count Ugolino, whose death in the
Tower of Hunger forms so horrible an episode in
the *Inferno* of Dante.  Reynolds had before this
entertained the intention of painting a picture from
the scene, and he proceeded, on the hint of Burke,
to produce what may be called his first historical
picture.  The design is well known by prints, and
has several elements of power.  The colour and
composition are impressive, but it required greater
gifts than Reynolds possessed to reach the tragic
height of a subject not very well suited to art.

It was while he was engaged on this work that
the University of Oxford conferred on him the
degree of Doctor of Civil Law, in companionship
with Dr. Beattie, whose portrait he painted soon

afterwards in gown and bands, holding his book
on Truth, as the Vicar of Wakefield might hold
*his* book on the Whistonian Controversy, while
the Angel of Justice or Truth is thrusting down
into darkness personifications of Infidelity and
Scepticism.   The figure of infidelity is made to
bear a strong resemblance to Voltaire, while that
of scepticism was said to resemble Hume.   This
treatment of the subject drew forth an indignant
protest from Goldsmith.   His objection was that
Beattie, as a writer, was so much the inferior of
Voltaire.   Whether this be a just objection or not,
there is surely great oddity in the combination of
a matter-of-fact clergyman, with gown and bands
and book, and the cloudy allegory in the back-
ground.   The mixture of real and allegorical
figures in Reynolds's picture of " Garrick between
Tragedy and Comedy," has been reasonably ob-
jected to ; but in this case there is more absurdity
in the combination, owing to the prosaic literal-
ness of the principal figure.

Sir Joshua's university honours were speedily
followed by a civic elevation, which he had long
coveted, and now much relished.   He is found at
Plympton going through the ceremony of being
sworn in as mayor of his native town.   It is said

that he was not without hope of taking his seat
in Parliament for the same place; but this never
came to pass.

Twenty-two years of unbroken prosperity had
passed over him.  His honours and emoluments
had reached their highest point.  He was no
longer to remain the unquestioned master of the
field of portraiture.  Three men of mark began to
make themselves felt in the world of art.

The first of these was James Barry, the son of
a Cork skipper, now over thirty years old, and
recently returned from Rome, where he had been
sent by Edmund Burke, whose conduct to him
raises Burke in our esteem.  Barry was a man
of great genius, but of unequal powers—fierce,
gloomy, misanthropic, opinionated, sarcastic, and
proud, with high views of the functions of art, and
large powers of invention, but failing in pictorial
knowledge and taste.  The second was Thomas
Gainsborough.  For some years past Wilshire's
waggon had brought from Bath, where Gainsborough had since 1760 resided, noble landscapes
and spirited portraits to the exhibition at Spring
Gardens.  These pictures secured high recognition
in London.  The painter of them was only four
years younger than Sir Joshua, had studied in

early life under Gravelot, the engraver, and Hayman, the painter, had met with good success at
Ipswich and Bath as a portrait painter, and now
resolved to set up his easel in the metropolis.
He rented a part of the Duke of Schomberg's
house in Pall Mall, for which he paid £300 a
year, and shortly became more popular than Reynolds. The more moderate scale of his prices
would no doubt contribute to this result ; but he
had a facility of pencil, an elegance, originality,
and spirit of execution, which made some of his
best portraits equal to some of the best works of
Sir Joshua. In addition he had powers which
Reynolds had not. Some of his landscapes are
among the masterpieces of art; and in certain of
his fancy subjects—cottage girls, woodmen, shepherd boys—there is a freshness and poetic power
never reached by Reynolds. Yet so overshadow-
ing and deeply rooted were the fame and influence
of Reynolds, that it was not till the gathering of
the Treasures of Art at Manchester, in 1857, that
the full relative value of Gainsborough's works
was seen by the British public. Reynolds had a
hold on the whole life of his age which Gainsborough never attained. His habits were different
from those of Reynolds. Not particularly well

educated, he was shy, sensitive, fond of home,
fond of music ; he mixed little in general society,
and never sought the company of the wits, or men
of learning.   For all that, he stands before us as
the more specific type of the man of genius both
by gifts and habitudes.

There was another rival in the field, whose
natural powers were probably of a higher cast
than those of either Reynolds or Gainsborough.
George Romney was born in 1734, in Lancashire,
and was brought up to his father's trade as a
cabinet-maker.   He had few educational advantages.   He studied portraiture under a country
artist, Steele, in Kendal, and for five years practised there with great success.   In 1762 he came
to London, and began to paint portraits at the
price of four guineas, which, by 1793, had risen
to thirty-five guineas.   From 1773 to 1775 he
studied in Italy, and after his return his popular-
ity as a portrait painter, though he did not after
1772 exhibit publicly, was unbounded.   Romney
was a friend of Flaxman the sculptor, and of
Hayley and Cowper, unequally matched poets.
His mode of execution was very simple.   He was
a good colourist, but did not aim at the fulness,
richness, and depth of Reynolds.   He had amaz-

F

ing power of striking in the forms of his subjects
at once, and had altogether more elevation of
thought and elasticity of fancy than Reynolds.
He never did himself full justice in the walk
where his powers were highest; but his "Shakespeare nursed by Tragedy and Comedy," his
Titanias, and some of the heads for which Lady
Hamilton was a frequent model, stand among the
very first things in English art, and suggest possibilities far beyond anything he ever had the full
opportunity of realising on canvas. "His heads,"
says Flaxman, a high authority, "were various.
The male were decided and grand, the female
lovely. His figures resembled the antique, the
limbs were elegant and finely formed, his drapery
well understood; few artists since the fifteenth
century have been able to do so much in so many
branches."

Reynolds had no longer the monopoly of portraiture, and we find from Northcote that from
that time he was not much employed in this way.
Henceforth he devoted more attention to fancy
subjects; but his fortune was made. He had
secured a position in society and among the
learned at which his rivals never aimed,
and he was upborne to the end of his days

at the highest point of reputation in his profession.

Goldsmith died in the year 1774. Johnson was turning his pen to the defence of the government of Lord North, and was writing *Taxation no Tyranny*. But the House of Assembly did not believe this; the sharp echo of rifles among the woods of Lexington was heard in England, and then the guns of Bunker's Hill; and the years of the American War passed stormily on, complicated with dangers nearer home. Paul Jones, on the northern coast, and the fleets of France in the south, threatened and alarmed the country. Sir Joshua turned out with Garrick to visit the camps; finding possibly that his sitters were few and his pursuits more solitary. The trial of Keppel and his acquittal, which set the town into a blaze of illumination, and drove the younger Pitt to the breaking of windows in his excitement, drew forth a letter of sympathy from Reynolds to his early friend, not now the young commodore, but the veteran admiral, of whom Burke wrote in after years so feelingly, and whose honest face was elevated to the dignity of innumerable signboards, long since rotted and fallen, while Sir Hugh Palisser was burnt in effigy.

Art, however, even under the frown of threatened
invasion, did not stand still. The exhibition was
removed from Spring Gardens to Somerset House,
where it remained down to our own time. Reynolds painted a not very excellent figure of
Theory sitting on a cloud, for the ceiling of the
new room. Two of his finest portrait groups,
those of the members of the Dilettanti Society,
were done in these years; and the designs for the
great window of Oxford, afterwards rendered in
glass, by Jervas—the Nativity in the centre, the
Virtues in various compartments. Some of the
designs for this series have been highly prized,
and were sold for large sums after his death.
The Nativity was bought by the young Duke of
Rutland, and was unfortunately burnt at the
great fire at Belvoir Castle, together with many
other fine works, one of which was a full length
portrait of General Oglethorpe, of Savannah. In
1780 he again visited Devonshire. He spent a
little time with Keppel at Bagshot, and with Dunning at Spitchwick-on-Dartmoor, while Burke
was making an unsuccessful appeal to his Bristol
constituency, and awarding unmeasured praise
to Dunning. Barry had enshrouded his gloomy
head in the Adelphi, which he had engaged to

decorate for nothing, living hardly for seven years,
and earning a scanty support by etching and
engraving by lamplight,—a noble instance of
devotion to art. The Adelphi Exhibition was
thrown open in 1783, and we find Dr. Johnson
present at the private view, and delivering the
dictum, "Here we see a grasp of mind that we
find nowhere else."

In 1781 Sir Joshua paid that visit to the Low
Countries, the result of which appeared in his published notes—a very valuable series of criticisms
on individual pictures.

His power had not declined, though he was
now sixty years of age. Indeed, the study of the
Flemish schools seemed to give new stimulus to
his mind and hand, and to the last there *was* no
decline in his power.

We cannot stay to look at Reynolds's political
opinions, or at the political changes from this
time: the Coalition ministry, the story of Fox's
*Martyrs*, the general elections, where Mrs. Crewe
(whose portrait as St. Geneviève among her sheep
is one of Sir Joshua's masterpieces) and the
Duchess of Devonshire mingled in the crowd;
nor at the passion for ballooning, of which Dr.
Johnson grew so tired of hearing. Over the

brave and grand career of Johnson the glooms
of the grave were spreading.   His health had
received severe shocks.   Hearing of the death of
Allan Ramsay, a good portrait painter, and a
learned and accomplished man, all his life a
friend both of Johnson and Reynolds, he writes :
"Whichever way I look, mortality presents its
formidable frown"; and soon the frown darkened
over his own head.   In patient submission and
devout contemplations, fixed on those great truths
of Christianity which he thought it almost profanity to defend by argument, his great voice
ceased—on Monday, 13th December 1784.   "Dr.
Johnson dyed at 7 in the afternoon," is the entry
in the pocket-book of Reynolds.

There are other events of much interest in the
years that remain, but the bright circlet of stars
was broken and obscured—Goldsmith, Beauclerk,
Garrick, Johnson, were all gone.   Sterne had
vanished suddenly long before.   From the flush
and glare of society he had found his way through
the gloom of a parish burying-ground, and the
sack of a body-snatcher, to the hideous resur-
rection of a Cambridge dissecting-table.   Boswell
was left lamenting and maudlin; untaught by all
his opportunities, and yet engaged on the best

biography in the world. " We are not sure," says
Macaulay, "that there is in the whole history of
the human intellect so strange a phenomenon as
this book. Many of the greatest men that ever
lived have written biography. Boswell was one
of the smallest men that ever lived, and he has
beaten them all."

Reynolds was not the man to succumb to the
dreary privations of age. As he lost his old
friends he did not close up his affections. He
had taken the poet Crabbe, in 1783, to supply
the void left by the death of Goldsmith ; and we
find him visiting and holding friendly intercourse
with a new race of amateurs and men of fashion,
such as Sir George Beaumont and Sir Abraham
Hume. To the years between 1784 and 1789,
too, belong the largest and most ambitious of
his works : the Infant Hercules, painted for the
Empress Catherine of Russia, who rewarded him
with a letter, a diamond snuff-box, and fifteen
hundred pounds, paid to his executors ; the Death
of Cardinal Beaufort, and Macbeth and the
Witches, for the Boydell gallery ; the Continence
of Scipio, also purchased by the Empress of
Russia ; and Cymon and Iphigenia, shown in the
International Exhibition of 1862, and one of his

finest works.    He also did some of his best
portraits in these few last years : John Hunter
and Joshua Sharp were among the number.
Two strokes of palsy had not disabled him either
in mind or body.    The year 1789, when he was
sixty-six years old, found him more passionately
in love with his palette and pencils than ever.

Miss Palmer, one of the two nieces who for
many years had kept his house, writes in 1787 :
" He is painting from morning to night, and the
truth is, that every picture he does seems better
than the former."    In power of execution, at any
rate, this was true.    The wonderful group of
" Cherub-heads," in our National Gallery, was
painted in 1787, and they are hardly exceeded, if
they are exceeded, in magic of touch by any heads
that were ever painted.

Till Monday, 13th July 1789, he worked with
untiring vigour.    On that day, as he was painting
the portrait of Miss Russell, " a mist and a darkness " fell over his left eye, " a dim suffusion
veiled " it, and from the same cause as in the case
of Milton, *gutta serena*.    He paused a moment,
gently laid down his pencil and his palette, and
resumed them no more.

" The race is over," he writes to Sheridan six

months afterwards, "whether it is won or lost."
He lived till the 23rd of February 1792. He
was often low-spirited, from fear of utter blind-
ness, but this did not come upon him. He
rambled to various scenes in quest of change and
health. He amused himself for a while with a
canary that used to perch on his hand and sing
to. him, but it proved faithless and flew away.
He wandered about Leicester Square after it for
hours, but did not find it. Ozias Humphry, the
painter, used to drop in and read the newspaper
to him, and he now and then retouched and
arranged his pictures, or slowly prepared his final
Discourse. This, the fifteenth, was delivered on
the 10th of December 1790 : "Sir Joshua had
a crowded audience, and while he was speaking,
a sudden crash was heard, and the floor of the
room seemed to be giving way. The company
rushed towards the door in the utmost alarm and
confusion. Sir Joshua was silent, and did not
move from his seat, and after some little time the
company perceiving that the danger had ceased,
most of them resumed their places, and he continued his discourse as calmly as if nothing had
occurred. It was afterwards found that one of
the beams which supported the floor had given

way. Sir Joshua remarked to Northcote, that if
the floor had really fallen, most of the persons
assembled must have been crushed to death, and
the arts in this country would have been thrown
two hundred years back."

The latter part of this memorable discourse
consists of a eulogium on Michael Angelo—its
last passage: "I reflect, not without vanity, that
these discourses bear testimony of my admiration
of that truly divine man, and I should desire
that the last words I should pronounce in this
Academy, and from this place, might be the name
of MICHAEL ANGELO."

"As Reynolds descended from the chair, Burke
stepped forward, and taking his hand, held it
while he addressed him in the words of Milton :—

"The angel ended, and in Adam's ear
So charming left his voice, that he awhile
Thought him still speaking, still stood fixed to hear.

"This I heard from Mr. Rogers, who said,
'Nobody but Burke could have done such a
thing, without its appearing formal or theatrical.
But from him it seemed spontaneous and irresistible. Such a tribute from such a man, formed
a fitting close for the life's work of Reynolds.'"

The disease of which Sir Joshua died was an affection of the liver, and this led to "a distressing depression of the spirits, which his physicians ascribed to hypochondria." Boswell, in a melancholy letter to his friend Temple, dated 22nd November 1791, says : "My spirits have been still more sunk by seeing Sir Joshua Reynolds almost as low as myself. He has for more than two months past had a pain in his blind eye, the effect of which has been to occasion a weakness in the other, and he broods over the dismal apprehension of becoming quite blind. He has been kept so low as to diet, that he is quite relaxed and desponding. He who used to be looked upon as perhaps the most happy man in the world, is now as I tell you."

Miss Burney, just released from the honours of court life and the talons of Madame Schwellenberg, called to see him. "He wore a bandage over one eye, and the other shaded with a green half-bonnet. He seemed serious even to sadness, though extremely kind. 'I am very glad,' he said, in a meek voice and dejected accent, 'to see you again, and I wish I could see you better, but I have but one eye now and scarcely that.'"

He bore patiently his last affliction, and died
as sincerely regretted as any man of his time.
While he lay dying, the political horizon was
dark and troubled, like one of those wild back-
grounds which we see in his portraits of warriors.
The first hot blasts of the French Revolution had
blown, but he did not live to see the final bursting
of the storm.    The next morning, in the house
where Sir Joshua lay, Edmund Burke wrote the
following obituary notice, which we cannot refrain
from quoting at length :—

*Last night*, in the sixty-ninth year of his age, died,
at his house in Leicester-fields, Sir Joshua Reynolds.
His illness was long, but borne with a mild and
cheerful fortitude, without the least mixture of anything irritable or querulous, agreeably to the placid
and even tenor of his whole life.   He had from the
beginning of his malady a distinct view of his dis-
solution, and he contemplated it with that entire
composure, which nothing but the innocence, integrity,
and usefulness of his life, and an unaffected submission to the will of Providence could bestow.   In this
situation he had every consolation from family tenderness, which his own kindness had indeed well de-
served.

Sir Joshua Reynolds was, on very many accounts,
one of the most memorable men of his time.   He was

the first Englishman who added the praise of the
elegant arts to the other glories of his country.  In
taste, in grace, in facility, in happy invention, and in
the richness and harmony of colouring, he was equal
to the great masters of the renowned ages.  In portrait he went beyond them ; for he communicated to
that description of the art, in which English artists
are the most engaged, a variety, a fancy, and a
dignity derived from the higher branches, which even
those who professed them in a superior manner ·did
not always preserve when they delineated individual
nature.  His portraits remind the spectator of the
invention of history, and the amenity of landscape.
In painting portraits he appeared not to be raised
upon that platform, but to descend to it from a
higher sphere.  His paintings illustrate his lessons,
and his lessons seem to be derived from his paintings.

He possessed the theory as perfectly as the
practice of his art.  To be such a painter, he was
a profound and penetrating philosopher.

In full affluence of foreign and domestic fame,
admired by the expert in art and by the learned in
science, courted by the great, caressed by sovereign
powers, and celebrated by distinguished poets, his
native humility, modesty, and candour, never forsook
him even on surprise or provocation, nor was the
least degree of arrogance or assumption visible to the
most scrutinising eye in any part of his conduct or
discourse.

His talents of every kind, powerful from nature, and not meanly cultivated by letters, his social virtues in all the relations and all the habitudes of life, rendered him the centre of a very great and unparalleled variety of agreeable societies, which will be dissipated by his death.   He had too much merit not to excite some jealousy; too much innocence to provoke any enmity.   The loss of no man of his time can be felt with more sincere, general, and unmixed sorrow.

### HAIL! AND FAREWELL!

His body lay in state at the Royal Academy, and was followed to the grave by a concourse such as had rarely been seen before on such an occasion. The Dukes of Portland, Dorset, and Leeds, the Marquises of Townshend and Abercorn, the Earls of Carlisle, Inchiquin, and Upper Ossory, Lord Palmerston, and Lord Elliot, bore his pall; and perhaps in the long list of mourners there has seldom been in a state funeral so many who would really mourn.   So lived, so died, so in "this kind of observance," was honoured the first renowned British artist—and one of the great artists of the world—standing in the front rank along with Titian, and Vandyke, and Rembrandt.

The contemplation of Reynolds's portraits is

one of the enjoyments of every highly-cultivated
Englishman. There is in them a calm dignity, a
bright life, a bewitching grace.

Mr. Taylor seems to be much impressed with
the "momentary" character of Reynolds's portraits.
What rapidity of eye, what accuracy of impression,
what spirit and sparkle of taste do we see in them.
Garrick with his thumbs pressed together, and
his conversational pertinence of look. Hunter
with his drooping pen and far wandering eye,

> Voyaging through strange seas of thought alone.

Banks with his instinctive restless desire to rise
from his chair and explore the earth to its utmost
horizons. And this *zest* runs through so many of
his portraits. How he got such endless variety
is a continual wonder. "Hang it, how *various* he
is!" said Gainsborough, as he paced the exhibition
rooms. We know the character of our "portrait
of a gentleman"; our corporation pictures; our
too dazzling Lord Mayors, before we see them;
the hot, encumbered appurtenances, the Boswellian
strut. But Reynolds's men, though boiling over
with action and motion, never strut. Their legs
are not always well drawn, but they do not stand
at ridiculous angles. If he stole all these viva-

cious attitudes, he was at least a most accomplished thief,—" *Convey* the wise it call." This rapid and consummate taste, this instinctive avoidance of " the weak side of things," this instant power of knowing when the right thing was before him, singles out Reynolds from all others.

See with what light and gallant spirit, yet with how little of the " bounce " of the modern " portrait of a gentleman," the Marquis of Hastings stands with his finger on his chin. See, in one of the ordinary run of his portraits, with what inquisitive ease John Gawler, Esquire, looks out of the kit-cat canvas ; with what negligent grace Captain Pownall leans on his anchor-fluke. How elegantly Lady Sondes sits on her garden seat, attractive and not a dowdy in spite of the black and white machinery on her head, that at first glance makes us somehow think irresistibly of earthquakes and tornadoes. And what for sumptuous naturalness and winning home-loveliness can exceed the long stately picture of Mrs. Wynne, and the children wrestling in each other's embraces ? His intense sense of life broke in among the preposterous costumes of his time. " Never mind," said he, " they have all light and shade." And even with such head-dresses, hat and feather, frizzy locks and fly-away ribbons, as we see in the portrait of Lady Lade, life triumphs, and constructions, puzzling for their immensity and complexity, are so broken with tender clouds and breezy trees and flitting shades, that all looks agreeable and natural.

The men who are everlastingly playing at backgammon and cards in the French Exhibition, in the restored costumes of the Reynolds period, look dull, and tiresome, and heavy, if better drawn than by Reynolds. But Reynolds does not make them dull and tiresome, and it shows his power. He "always looked on his picture as a whole,"—and how wonderful are the occult relations of line, colour, and effect which go to make up a whole picture! There seem to be in them hidden powers that baffle all analysis. It is not mere mass or extent that gives sublimity. Perhaps there is no picture more solemn in general effect than the "Peter Martyr" of Titian; none which, among other elements, gives so impressive a suggestion of forest grandeur; yet it is not accomplished by representing great masses of forest scenery. Let the spectator compare the size of the trees with the size of the figures, and he will find that all the materials of the scene,

G

with the exception of the sky and the piece of
distant mountain, might be contained inside a
room.   The nearest tree is not thicker than the
thigh of the assassin, and not more than fourteen
feet high.   Both trees might any day be passed
in a hedgerow, with a sense of their insignificance,
and the foreground is not more than ten feet wide.
It is the bend, the sway, the subservience, the
collocation, the mystery of relation to the human
and divine interest of the scene, that makes them
what they are.   Man, as seen by the painter's
eye, is seen in certain compressed conditions.
The men we see apart from the framings and
contrivances, and limitations of art, are puzzlingly
little.   Across a street we can just recognise a
face and figure.   Seen against the great back-
grounds of nature, man is nothing.   The generalissimo ruling among thunderclouds, and making
the mountains bow on the canvas of Reynolds,
is a speck out of doors.   The greatest battle seen
from the hill-brow is but the waving of " thin red
lines " in a smoky field.   Take the man as he
could be made to fit against the cloud or the rock,
and his importance dwindles—he has no " relief."
There was smoke and roar at Gibraltar; the roar
only terrific within a league.   No one saw General

Elliott's head as we see it in the picture in the
National Gallery, standing out, with its triangular
obstinate eyebrows, against the twisting clouds
and the down-pointing gun. Man has to dignify
*himself*, and to the great painter who can do it for
him as Reynolds could, he will willingly accord
"ceremonies of bravery even in the infamy of his
nature." This vast desire of man Reynolds was
able to gratify. He rendered with equal perception and ease the politician in his robes of office ;
the mighty noble in velvet and ermine ; the wit,
with his jest simmering on his features ; the
student poring over his book, with near and piercing regard, as Baretti and Johnson, or looking afar
with contemplative serenity like Zachary Mudge ;
the country gentleman with his favourite dog,
enjoying the repose of a rustic seat in the shade
of his ancestral beech tree, in the gray afternoon,
like Sir John Lade ; the *dilettante* fingering his
gem or his gem-like glass of wine; the man of
pleasure taking it with easy grace ; the fashionable
beauty pillowed in state, with her gray towers of
curl and plaster and plume, or tripping under
narrow trees that bend to make her bending more
graceful ; the actress in tragic state, like Mrs.
Yates or Mrs. Siddons; in saucy surprises, like

Mrs. Abington ; or in the mere lazy luxury of
living, like Kitty Fisher, or "my Lady O'Brien";
or, sweetest of all, the little children! It was in
these that Reynolds reaches farthest into the
heart. We melt before the picture of "Innocence,"
with her dimpled hands on her bosom. We are
hushed before the infant Samuel, who yet is only
a modern child, "called of the Lord"—sacred
enough as such. There is a throng of these little
ones peering at us from canvas and canvas, calling
us back to our childhood with winning smiles and
wondering eyes. In doing these his power seemed
to rise with age. Let any one look well, who has
not already often looked, at those cherub heads,
all done from little Lady Mary Gordon, and
painted not long before " the drop serene " brought
him to a final pause : praised by Leslie for its
exquisite evanescent touch and pure colour, but
rising far beyond all technical grace. If we search
anywhere among " the figures of the true " for an
illustration of the words, " for of such is the
kingdom of heaven," let us see it there. It is as
much sermon as art can yield, simply to bring
together before the mind's eye this picture and
the Kitty Fishers and Nelly O'Briens, and make
no further comment.

The greatest of all Reynolds's achievements in
portraiture was the portrait of Mrs. Siddons, as
Tragedy, on her cloudy throne.  In this instance,
the strange and ugly fashion in which the hair at
that period was dressed, rather aids than impedes
the sentiment.  The whole mass moves horrent
from the brow as if standing on end; the dark
eyebrows rise under it in slight corrugation, and
the springs of imagination are moved.  " Scaffolds,
still sheets of water, divers woes," the collapse of
power, the eclipse of nations, terror, and the
immensity of human sorrow, pass in twilight
procession as we look, and haunt us when we turn
away.

On the force, and dignity, and life, and naturalness of his portraits, there was, as his most peculiar
distinction, the crown of *grace*.  He was, as Ruskin
happily calls him, " lily-sceptred."  Taken by
itself, and apart from science, we might almost
say that Raphael himself had no higher sense of
grace.  We pardon even his incorrectness in the
bewitching fluency of this element in his female
portraits.  It reached to the disposition of a curl
and the flow of a fold.  That and the sense of life
and motion which pervades his pictures carry us
away, and do not even suffer us long to weary

of his works. And it was just that exquisitely
balanced mixture of outward practical sense and
spirit, with the amenity of a graceful soul, that
made him so beloved in society, so able to please,
without flattery or loss of independence. We can
see for ourselves the refutation of Allan Cunningham's insinuations; he had no need of the smooth
tongue of the courtier to secure his success. He
had a happy mixture of wisdom and gentleness—

> Still born to improve us in every part ;
> His pencil our faces, his manners our heart.

Where Reynolds fell into the unhappy classic
vein of his time, it is impossible to relish many
of his works ; they become oppressive. Compare
the dress of Mrs. Braddyl, its lively accidental
" set," or the attire of the Ladies Waldegrave, in
that lovely group where two are winding silk, and
one is embroidering at a real table, with a drawer
and a key, and think of their being exchanged for
"The Graces adorning a bust of the Duchess as
Magna Mater" — the Graces with great *têtes*
pomatumed and powdered, the Graces in stays,
the Graces without hoops, but with dresses lashed
about their legs in . such a manner as only the
wettest and thinnest muslin would cling in the

wildest storms, yet doing it, defiant of law, in the
profoundest calm! "What," says Uncle Toby,
"has a man who believes in God to do with these
things?" Let the Graces wander in Ionia as
Praxiteles saw them, and teach what they could
to a world that "by wisdom knew not God." Our
great-grandmothers, playing at Graces, and cook-
ing sacrifices to perished divinities, "swearing by
the sin of Samaria, and saying, Thy god, O Dan,
liveth, and the manner of Beersheba liveth," were
too much for even Reynolds to render tolerable
to a Christian age. One of the best of these we
can examine at our leisure in the National Gallery.
Three celebrated beauties are "adorning the altar
of Hymen," but, O that they had been winding
silk, or shooting at targets, or even occupied, as it
is said one fine lady who sat to him was—"eating
beefsteaks and playing at cricket on the Steyne,
at Brighton!"

Burke says that Reynolds seemed to descend to
portraiture from a higher sphere. It was from the
mount of philosophy that he descended, and not
from "the highest heaven of invention." There
was one thing he had not,—the perception of the
unseen, of the something beyond. "Great and
graceful as he paints," he is "a man of the earth,"

seeing, it is true, all that is noblest and best on
"this visible diurnal sphere," but never quitting
it. In one instance—the portrait of Mrs. Siddons
—we just feel the inflation of the balloon. It
strains, and rocks, but it does not leave the ground.
It was Mrs. Siddons more than Sir Joshua who
gave the spiritual element to it. Other men of
his time had the gift. Fuseli had it. In spite of
Horace Walpole, with his lace ruffles and his two
strokes of catalogue-disdain, Fuseli makes us feel
the Gothic thrill at ghostly evanescence, the gray
gliding mysteries of Hercynian forests, the stalk of
mailed phantoms—

> By thy wild and stormy steep,
>               Elsinore.

If he saw no gods descend from heaven, he saw
them in the caverns of Endor "rising out of the
earth." If he could not soar and blaze with Uriel,
he could sink by thought into the profound of
Hades, and see the cloudy gates of Chaos and the
pit, and the key that was "forged by no earthly
smith." We feel his spell creeping in the roots
of the hair. "Nature put him out," but he *saw*
what he tried to paint if he could not perfectly
paint all that he saw.

And Romney, too, had the great gift. But it was the Greek gift, and not the Scandinavian. He beheld the Oread on her mountain heath, the Naiad by her ferny wells, the wild prevision of Cassandra, the stony horror of Œdipus waiting for his doom. And Gainsborough had it, but it was the true British imagination that possessed *him*. It was that swelling, glowing, heavenly-solemn faculty, that dwelt in the author of *The Seasons*,

> For ever rising with the rising mind,

to which the cultured Englishman most readily responds, as he hears the sweep of autumnal gales in his own island, or through glades whose leafage is yellowing to the fall looks westward at his misty sunsets, exalted by the pleasing Miltonic melancholy with which he would " choose to live."

Reynolds had it *not*. He *fished for* such ideas as did not walk in the daylight. They never rose spontaneously from the deep, and the genii, caught by guile, sulk and are uneasy on his canvas. There is a touch of the terrible in the picture of Cardinal Beaufort, and we wish the anecdote of the grinning coalheaver who sat for it had been suppressed. Yet the anecdote only proves that Shakespeare himself in his awfully minute delineation could not quicken the sterile fancy of Reynolds without the help of the coalheaver.

In the highest subjects of all, his failure was the most signal. Of the Oxford window, our only intuition is, that it is abominable in theory, in conception, in style. The lubberly angel above, the smirking faces below, the vapid rows of Virtues between the mullions, scarcely higher in invention than those blindfold white women with scales, and idiotic Hopes with anchors, which support the dignity of a "Perpetual Grand Master" of the Order of Odd Fellows, on his engraved diploma,—are all bad together. It is a wonder that Reynolds should be so anxious to have his name "hitched in" in connection with so aimless, tasteless, and absurd an attempt. There were ten pictures under the great historic "Infant Hercules," "some better, some worse," he said, and there is something grand about the work, but not enough to kindle the mind. The "Macbeth" was a curious *réchauffé* of Verrio, Michael Angelo, and Sir Joshua Reynolds. Many of his purely *fancy* pictures are charming—his Shepherd Boys, Cupids in Disguise, Muscipulas,

Strawberry Girls, Contemplative Boys, Fortune
Tellers. Whatever he could reach by vision and
taste he could do, but the gates of imagination
were closed and sealed to him. It was his calling
to portray, and the allowance of his gifts was
large enough.

The chief praise which Mr. Taylor awards to
Reynolds's writings on art is, that "their tendency
is upwards." He had a strong conviction of the
high claims of art on the attention of thinking
men, and does not so much enforce this as assume
it. This is, after all, one of the chief uses of the
pen in the region of art. The medium of pictorial
art is not *words*. It would be possible to render
the most exact account in words of what a picture
ought to be, without having the least perception
of what it is, or the least power to judge it aright.
The most valuable practical utterances are the
simple dicta of great painters as to the relative
status and qualities of pictures. The moment
verbal analysis is attempted, the utter poverty of
language in *that* sphere is made apparent. The
finest criticisms are mere finger-posts to mark the
road on which they do not travel. Where a
painter takes the pen, however, he is amenable to
the pen. Reynolds was a pioneer in the direction

of statements on art.  The laws which govern art
—and here is one of its charms to those who
pursue it—are those common to all the great
pursuits of life.  "So close," writes Erskine, "is
the analogy between all the operations of genius,
that your Discourse is the best dissertation upon
the art of public eloquence that ever was or ever
will be written."  But, when these laws are discovered and laid down, the materials amongst
which they work, the phenomena of aspect, line,
form, colour, light, shade, effect, have all to be
learnt and understood before a man can become
a good critic of painting ; and the full meaning of
Reynolds's discourses, inaccurate as they may be in
some of their reasonings, may be misunderstood if
the painter and the literary critic do not intend
the same thing.  The true painter reasons with
his brush, and can afford but little leisure to help
forward that correct statement of the functions
and laws of art which, in a verbal form, enter little
into his meditations, but which yet are so much
to be desired as a common platform between the
artist and the man of general culture.  "The eye
has its own poetry," says Sir Charles Eastlake.

Reynolds's *methods* of painting were chiefly
useful to our school in the way of warning.

Many of his finest pictures are already blurred
and blighted beyond hope of recovery. His *aims*
as to colour and texture were not always satis-
factory. He used wax compounds, that now and
then go far to suggest Madame Tussaud or Mrs.
Jarley, in their confectionary surface. It was his
practice to lay in the likeness, in what is called
"dead colour," with little more than black and
white : over this, when dry, he passed transparent
varnishes and mixtures, charged with the tints
required to complete the colour. These colours
—carmines, lakes, and other vegetable hues—
were often fleeting. They "sparkled and exhaled"
under the power of sunshine. Sometimes the
varnish would turn brown or green, and ruin the
complexion. Sometimes a thick-headed cleaner
would fetch it all off, and find the *caput mortuum*
below. A still more fatal practice was to lay one
coat on another, with materials that had no blood
relationship, and then there were constant feuds
and insurrections among the pigments, and the
picture was rent asunder. "Oh, heavens! Murder!
Murder!" says the ranting Haydon, as he spells
out the comical occult recipes, partly broken
English and partly Italian, in which Sir Joshua
recorded these experiments. "Murder!—it would

crack under the brush!" His pictures have often
a very special charm, arising from what Haydon
calls "his glorious gemmy surface." This was in
part owing to the reflex influence of his want of
facility. There were ten pictures under "the
Infant Hercules," and many of his best pictures,
before he had done with them, had been so loaded
with coat on coat of rich pigments, rough and
intermingled with all the tints of the palette, that
they were ready for the final and magical
"surface" that enchanted Haydon. When the
full idea was seized, then came the "lily-sceptred"
hand, and the light brush in its graceful sweeps
catching the upper surfaces of the many-coloured
granules, permits the eye to see, through the
liberated airy stroke, the sparkle of the buried
wealth beneath. Romney struck in his forms
with masterly ease at once, even at the first sitting; and if in him we miss this jewelled richness,
it is abundantly compensated by the breathing
sense of power which plays around his works of
imagination.

Reynolds's personal character is fascinating.
If we are to judge of a man's worth by the rank
and style of his friends, what shall we say of the
man who secured such invariable and decided

testimonials from Samuel Johnson—of him whom
the author of the *Vicar of Wakefield* loved like a
brother? Let us first read Burke's eulogies on
Dunning and Keppel, and then reflect that Burke,
Dunning, and Keppel were among Sir Joshua's
most intimate friends. The terms used by all
who knew him in describing his manners are all
of one order. Calm, simple, unaffected, placid,
genial, gentle, are words of constant occurrence on
all sides in any attempt to characterise him.

In his mental organisation, the most prominent
faculty pointed at by all is the power of generalisation. "To be such a painter he was a profound
and penetrating philosopher." Mr. Taylor watches
closely his habit of "condensing" in conversation.
Then came that precious virtue of taste — the
guard of his rapid observation and intense sense
of character. His surprising *vitality*, which palsy
could only threaten, which age could not lower, is
to be very especially noticed. It was this that
permitted his life, "so full of labour that tongue
cannot utter it." His fruitfulness was not less
than *prodigious*.

We may pry too curiously into the *moral* of a
life, but no truly thoughtful person can omit all
consideration of it from his final judgment. This

consideration is especially provoked when the subject of it has been eminently fortunate and happy, and it is invited in the case of Sir Joshua Reynolds by the generalised conception he entertained of life *as a whole.* Did *all* the elements of calculation enter into his arrangement of "the great game he had to play"? He was convicted of nothing usually accounted a vice. In manners, in temper, he was all that could be wished or expected. He was—Dr. Johnson said—"invulnerable" as a member of civil society. He had respect for religion, as appears in various incidental ways. We are not informed if he were a churchgoer. We are told that he painted on Sunday, and that Johnson urged him to abandon the practice. His sister, Mrs. Palmer, was much concerned, and expostulated with him on the same subject. Johnson exhorted him to read the Bible daily, and to consider his latter end.

It is well that we are not called on to look to the life of a man for a standard of virtue and religion. That is found outside a man. But it is permitted to us, it is enjoined upon us, for *our own* improvement, encouragement, or warning, to judge of a man's conformity to that standard, and thus know him by his "fruits." In the case of those individual acts, which do not clearly contradict any known moral or divine law, the moral significance is indeed as hard to ascertain as it would be to pick out and protest against those parts of Reynolds's pictures which were painted on Sunday. We look with high respect on the religious spirit of Johnson, and we see him occasionally doing pretty much the same things that Reynolds did. At the theatre, the masquerade, at Ranelagh, at Vauxhall, in the company of wits and men of fashion, we find him by the side of Reynolds. We have much information as to the creed and religious habits of Johnson. We have none as to those of Sir Joshua, and we can only *ponder*.

## II

## WILLIAM BLAKE

THE great landscape painter, Linnell — whose
portraits were, some of them, as choice as
Holbein's—in the year 1827 painted a portrait
of William Blake, the great idealist, an engraving of which is before us as we write. A
friend, looking at it, observed that it was " like a
landscape." It was a happy observation. The
forehead resembles a corrugated mountain-side
worn with tumbling streams " blanching and
billowing in the hollows of it "; the face is twisted
into "as many lines as the new map with the
augmentation of the Indies"; it is a grand face
ably anatomised, full of energy and vitality, and
out of these labyrinthine lines there gazes an eye
which seems to behold things more than mortal.
At the Exhibition of National Portraits at South
Kensington there was a portrait of Blake by

Thomas Phillips; but very different in treatment:
the skin covers the bones and sinews more calmly,
the attitude is eager, wistful, and prompt. Comparing the two portraits, so fine and so different
in style and manner, you are able adequately to
conceive the man; and in both you feel that this
awful EYE, far-gazing, subduing the unseen to
itself, was the most wonderful feature of the
countenance. It is the countenance of a man
whose grave is not to be recognised at this day,
while Linnell lives on in venerable age producing
his glorious representations of the phenomena of
Nature as she appears out of doors, and, we
believe, enjoying a large success, which he would
merit, if for nothing else, as the reward of his
kindness to William Blake. On the title-page
of Gilchrist's *Life of William Blake* he is
characterised as *Pictor Ignotus*. It was
published in 1863, and he is "unknown" no
longer.[1] Even at this distance of time the topic
may have something of that mixture of old

---

[1] This essay was written as a review of the first edition of
the *Life of William Blake*, by A. Gilchrist. A part of it was afterwards reprinted in the second edition of that work edited by Mrs.
Gilchrist and D. G. Rossetti. It was thus introduced by the
latter: "Next among Blake-labours of love, let me here refer to
Mr. James Smetham's deeply sympathetic and assimilative study

and new which is more charming than either
taken separately, and assuredly such a life is not
to be classed among those things which are only
interesting while the flower of novelty is upon
them—for "the artist never dies."

If we wished by a single question to sound the
depth of a man's mind and capacity for the judgment of works of pure imagination, we know of
none we should be so content to put as this one,

(in the form of a review article on the present life), published in
the *London Quarterly Review* for January 1869.   As this article
is reprinted in our present Vol. II., no further tribute to its
delicacy and force needs to be made here : it speaks for itself.
But some personal mention, however slight, should here exist
as due to its author, a painter and designer of our own day who
is, in many signal respects, very closely akin to Blake ; more so
probably than any other living artist could be said to be.   James
Smetham's work—generally of small or moderate size—ranges
from Gospel subjects, of the subtlest imaginative and mental
insight, and sometimes of the grandest colouring, through Old
Testament compositions and through poetic and pastoral themes
of every kind to a special imaginative form of landscape.

" In all these he partakes greatly of Blake's immediate spirit,
being also often nearly allied by landscape intensity to Samuel
Palmer, who was in his youth the noble disciple of Blake.   Mr.
Smetham's works are very numerous, and, as other exclusive
things have come to be, will some day be known in a wide
circle.   Space is altogether wanting to make more than this
passing mention here of them and of their producer, who shares
in a remarkable manner Blake's mental beauties and his
formative shortcomings, and possesses besides an individual
invention which often claims equality with the great exceptional master himself."

" What think you of William Blake ? " He is one
of those crucial tests which at once manifest the
whole man of art and criticism. He is a stumbling-
block to all pretenders, to all conventional learned-
ness, to all merely technical excellence. Many a
notorious painter whose canvases gather crowds
and realise hundreds of pounds, might be, as it
were, detected and shelved by the touch of this
" officer in plain clothes." In him there is an
utter freedom from pretence. Mr. Thackeray,
with all his minute perception of human weak-
nesses and meannesses, could not have affixed upon
this son of nature any, the smallest, accusation of
what he has called " snobbishness." As soon
might we charge the west wind or the rising
harvest moon or the gray - plumed nightingale
with affectation as affix the stigma upon this
simple, wondering, child - man, who wanders in
russet by " the shores of old romance," or walks
" with death and morning on the silver horns " in
careless and familiar converse with the angel of
the heights. You may almost gather so much if
you only look on the engraved portrait. Say if
that upright head, sturdy as Hogarth's, sensitive as
Charles Lamb's, dreamy and gentle as Coleridge's,
could ever have harboured a thought either

malignant or mean ?   It is a recommendation to
the biography.  He must have a dull soul indeed
who, having seen that face, does not long to know
who and what the man was who bore it ; and it
shall be our endeavour, in our humble way, to act
as a guide to the solution of the inquiry.  But
before giving some account of "who," it must
be permitted to offer some preliminary reflec-
tions, enabling us better to understand "what"
he was.

No question in art or literature has been more
discussed and with less decisiveness than that of
the relations of subject-matter to style or form ;
and on the view taken by the critic of the comparative value of these relations will depend the
degree of respect and admiration with which he
will regard the products of Blake's genius.  To
those who look on the flaming inner soul of
invention as being of far more importance than
the grosser integuments which harbour and defend
it, giving it visibility and motion to the eye,
Blake will stand on one of the highest summits
of excellence and fame.  To those who, having
less imagination and feeling, are only able to
comprehend thought when it is fully and perfectly
elaborated in outward expression, he must ever

seem obscure, and comparatively unlovely. There
can be no doubt that the true ideal is that which
unites in equal strength the forming and all-
energising imagination, and the solid body of
external truth by which it is to manifest itself to
the eye and the mind.

There are moments when the sincere devotee
of Blake is disposed to claim for him a place as
great as that occupied by Michael Angelo; when,
carried away by the ravishment of his fiery wheels,
the thought is lost beyond the confines of sense,
and he seems "in the spirit to speak mysteries."
In more sober hours, when it is evident that we
are fixed for the present in a system of embodi-
ment which soul informs but does not blur or
weaken or obscure, we are compelled to wish that
to his mighty faculty of conception Blake had
added that scientific apprehensiveness which,
when so conjoined, never fails to issue in an
absolute and permanent greatness. But having
granted thus much, let us not spoil one of the
most original and charming of the many joys to
be found "in stray gifts to be claimed by whoever
shall find" along the meads of art, by hankering
after what will not be found, or quarrelling with
what we cannot mend. Before we can come to

a true initiation into, and an abiding enjoyment of, the domains of representative art, we must have a keen, clear, settled, and contented view of its *limitations*. Far less of the fruitlessness of discontent enters into poetry and literature than into the subject of painting and sculpture. One would think that the reason of this was obvious, yet it is lost sight of continually. Our experience has shown us that there are few who receive from works of a plastic kind a tithe of their power to please because of the narrow, uncatholic, querulous condition of mind arising from a false standard and unwarrantable expectations. They will not be at the pains to recollect the wide chasm of difference between a medium in which only that need be told which can be told with truth, and one in which *all* must be told, either truthfully or untruthfully; they will not reflect that the visible phenomena of nature are endless; that absolute perfection requires the presence of the whole series of those phenomena, and that nothing less can produce on the eye the full effect of nature ; that the conditions on which representations are made are subject to such an infinity of accidents, that it would take a regiment rather than a single man to catch the mere blush and bloom of any

one aspect of nature at any one time. They forget
that life is short, health variable, opportunity
mutable, means precarious, memory feeble, days
dark, " models " impracticable, pigments dull, and
media disappointing.

Let us implore the visitor of gallery and studio
to reflect for a while on these inexorable limitations and distinctions, and to endeavour rather to
extract pleasure out of what is absolutely *there*
than to repine over the lack of sufficiencies which
probably, if demanded, would be found as incom-
patible with the subject treated as to paint the
creaking of a gibbet or the shriek of a steam-
whistle. For our own part, with any such persons
we should hesitate until this investigation had
been comprehensively and satisfactorily made, to
draw forth on a winter evening and in the sober
quiet of the study, where alone such an action
should be performed, that plain, grand, and solemn
volume which is called *Illustrations of the Book of
Job*, invented and engraved by William Blake.
And we should even longer hesitate before we
called his enthusiastic attention to the small,
rather rude and dark-looking, but to our mind
most precious facsimile of the book which is
appended to Gilchrist's *Life of Blake*. And yet

our inward thought on the subject is that in the
whole range of graphic art there is no epic more
stately, no intellectual beauty more keen and
thrilling, no thinking much more celestial and
profound.

The history and career of the designer of this
noble poem are as interesting as his work. Judged
by the ridiculous standard most frequently used
in England for the admeasurement of position his
life was unsuccessful and his surroundings mean.
Judged by that far more exalted scale which
Wordsworth applies when he praises the " plain
living and high thinking " of former ages and
men, his life was enviable and serene, a confluence
of outward sufficiency and inward wealth ample
enough to have stored a hundred minds.

He was born in November 1757 in Broad
Street, Carnaby Market, Golden Square. His
father was a hosier in moderate circumstances,
who gave him but an imperfect education. He
was a dreamy child, and fond of rambling into the
country, to Blackheath, Norwood, and Dulwich.
His faculties and proclivities were soon enough
seen, and in startling forms. He not only imagined,
but said that he actually *saw* angels nestling in
a tree and walking among the haymakers in a field.

In these country rambles we have one of the germs of his peculiar character and genius. Human powers and opportunities act and react on each other. The fledgling bird has enfolded in its bosom the passion for flight and for song, and, one might think, realises by foretaste, as the winds rock its nest, the music of the woods and the rapture of the illimitable air. So there are premonitory stirrings as sweet and inexpressible in the breast of the heaven-made child of genius. They are its surest sign. Talent grows insensibly, steadily, and discreetly. Genius usually has in early years a joyous restlessness, a keen, insatiable relish of life ; an eye soon touched with the "fine frenzy," and glancing everywhere. It is—

> Nursed by the waterfall
> That ever sounds and shines,
> A pillar of white light upon the wall
> Of purple cliffs aloof descried ;

and is as various, as incessant, as full of rainbow colour and mingled sound. One of our most unquestionable men of genius tells us how, as a child, landscape nature was effectually haunted to him. The cataract chimed in his ears and sang mysterious songs, the "White Lady of Avenel" fluttered about his path or sank in the black swirl and foam of the whirlpool. A child-painter will find it a bliss to notice that the distant hills are of a fine Titianesque blue long before he knows who Titian was or has seen a picture. It will give him ineffable joy to see how the valley lifts itself towards the mountains and how the streams meander from their recesses. He is not taught this; it comes to him as blossoms come to the spring, and is the first mark of his vocation. It was this inward thirst and longing that sent out the boy Blake into the fields and lanes and among the suburban hills. The force of boyish imagination must have been stronger in him than in most, even of the children of genius, for as early as the age of thirteen or fourteen the conceptions of his mind began to assume an external form. He saw a tree sparkling in the sun, and discovered that it was *filled with angels*. When he narrated this event at home his father was disposed to beat him for telling a lie, and would have done so but for the interposition of his mother; yet he continued to maintain the substantial truth of his story.

In later life he perplexed friends and strangers by this mingling of the inward and outward. He was on one occasion " talking to a little group gathered round him, within hearing of a lady whose children had just come home from boarding-school for the holidays. 'The other evening,' said Blake, in his usual quiet way, 'taking a walk, I came to a meadow, and at the farther corner of it I saw a fold of lambs. Coming nearer, the ground blushed with flowers, and the wattled cote and its woolly tenants were of an exquisite pastoral beauty. But I looked again, and it proved to be no living flock but beautiful sculpture.' The lady, thinking this was a capital holiday show for her children, eagerly interposed, 'I beg your pardon, Mr. Blake, but *may* I ask *where* you saw this?' '*Here*, madam,' answered Blake, touching his forehead. The reply brings us to the point of view from which Blake himself regarded his visions. It was by no means the mad view those ignorant of the man have fancied. He would candidly confess that they were not literal matters of fact, but phenomena seen by his imagination, *realities* none the less for that, but transacted within the realm of mind."

We must say that there is something baffling in this double-minded assertion. That ideas in " the realm of mind," where the faculty of imagination is strong, become equivalent in importance to

realities, is never questioned ; it is a waste of our
interest and sympathy to claim for them more
than a mental life, since no end can be answered
by it, unless it be to suggest an unnecessary charge
of unsoundness of mind ; and, on the other hand,
the want of judgment displayed in thus uselessly
tampering with the feelings of others exposes a
man to a similar charge on different grounds.   But
even in regard to what is called vision by the
inward eye, there are certain limitations which
should not be forgotten.   Fuseli wished he could
" paint up to what he *saw*."   Other instances
have been heard of where this clearness of mental
vision was laid claim to, where, nevertheless, the
artist made abundance of various preparatory
sketches.   It might appear that if the interior
image does indeed possess the actual completeness
of life, there is nothing to do but copy what is
before the mind's eye.   There are painters of the
highest imagination who do not possess this extravagant sensibility and completeness of parts in
the regions of conception.   They have the animation of a labouring, inward idea which glimmers
before the vision.   They have judgment and taste
by which they know when it is successfully
translated into outward form.   But all the

greatest painters have referred to and depended most minutely on the aid of natural models for the whole series of facts by means of which the image was to be realised on canvas.

Young Blake's visions of angels, when analysed, would probably occur in some such way as the following :—It was in no green-topped suburban tree that he saw the heavenly visitants ; we must rather suppose him returning after the oxygen of the Surrey hill winds had exalted his nerves, among the orchards of some vale into which the last rays of the sun shine with their setting splendours. Here he pauses, leans over a gate, looks at a large, blossom-loaded tree in which the threads of sunlight are entangled like gossamers, which "twinkle into green and gold." A zephyr stirs the cloud of sun-stricken bloom, where white commingled with sparkling red flushes over leaves of emerald. Tears of boyish delight "rise from his heart, and gather to his eyes" as he gazes on it. The rays which kindle the blossoms turn his gathered tears to prisms, through which snow-white and ruby blooms, shaken along with the leaf-emeralds, quiver and dance. The impressible brain, already filled with thoughts of the "might of stars and angels," kindles suddenly into a

dream-like creative energy and the sunny orchard
becomes a Mahanaim, even to his outward eye.

So it must have been with that other similar
incident.    He rambles among hayfields where
white-robed girls, graceful as those whom Mulready
has represented in the haymaking scene in Mr.
Baring's gallery, are raking the fragrant fallen
grass, and singing as they move.    There are times
when men not particularly imaginative, looking
on the bloom of girlhood and softened by the
music of youthful voices, come very near to the
illusion by which the imagination raises "a mortal
to the skies," or draws "an angel down." Blake,
under the enchantments of boyhood and beauty,
only took the short remaining stride and fancy
became sufficiently veracious fact.

He began early to draw — attended picture
sales and frequented print shops—was "put to
Mr. Pars's drawing-school in the Strand," where
he copied casts from the antique, collected engravings from the great Italians and Germans, and
before he was fourteen began to compose poetry
of unwonted sweetness, and containing the germ
of that strange lyric power in which he stands
alone among lyrists.    It was one of the happy
circumstances of Blake's career that his parents

did not attempt to throw hindrances in the way
of his becoming an artist, since most men observe
with considerable anxiety any traces of special
inclination to the pursuit of art shown by their
children, because of the great uncertainty which,
no doubt, attaches to the calling.

A few words may here be worth setting down on
this head. Times have greatly altered in this, as
in so many other particulars, since Blake's day.
The whole field and apparatus of design have been
enlarged. In the year 1767 there was nothing
like the variety of occupation for the painter
which there is now. In those days the artist, like
the poet, had little chance of success unless he
were taken by the hand and " patronised," in the
old sense of the word. As the likelihood of being
thus noticed depended greatly on accident, it was
a dangerous risk for a lad to run when he resolved
on throwing his life into the pursuit of painting
or sculpture. Reynolds was so fortunate as to
obtain high patronage early in life, and was of a
constitution of mind able to use without abusing
his opportunities. Wilkie, when only twenty
years of age, gained the lifelong friendship and
support of Sir George Beaumont and Lord
Mulgrave. He, too, had that admiration for

I

grand society, and that placid and humble temper,
which promoted the stability of such aids to
success.  Jackson was found on a tailor's shop-
board by the same kindly and noble Lord
Mulgrave, and was allowed £200 a year to enable
him to study, until it became evident such good
fortune was ruining him, and then the annuity
was mercifully withdrawn.  No doubt many
young painters who have never made their way
in life have been "taken up" by eminent patrons.
Patronage will not qualify a painter though the
want of it may prevent the highest abilities from
being fairly developed.  It is questionable whether
even the best early patronage would have enabled
Blake to succeed in any high degree.  We shall
see as we proceed that the inherent qualities of
his mind—the marked and settled characteristics
of his work, chosen and cultivated with a strength
of conviction which no opinion of others, no baits
of fortune, no perception of self-interest, could
have shaken or disturbed—these, as well as the
quality of his temper, were such that he never
could have been largely appreciated during his
own life.  In so far as he becomes more and more
recognised, it will be through a medium of interpretation, partly literary, partly artistic, which

will enable thoughtful and refined minds to read
his works as they read the classics in the dead
languages. The lapse of a century has altered all
the external conditions of art. There is no longer
a need for patronage in the ancient sense of the
word. No painter has to take his turn in Lord
Chesterfield's anteroom—pictured for us by E. M.
Ward—with the yawning parson who comes to
dedicate his volume of sermons, the widow who
wants a place in the charity-school for her son,
the wooden-legged, overlooked, sea-captain who
indignantly lugs out his turnip of a chronometer,
the insolent, red-coated man of the turf who peers
through an eye-glass fixed on the end of his jockey-
whip at the frowning and impatient Samuel
Johnson in snuff-colour who is perhaps even now
chewing the bitter cud of that notable sentence
which begins, "Is not a patron my Lord?" and
ends with the words "encumbers him with help."

It is comparatively rarely that an English
noble buys the more precious work of the pencil.
The men to whom the painter addresses himself
with hope are the wealthy merchant, the successful tradesman, the tasteful lawyer, the physician
in good practice. While pushing up to the higher
levels, most young men of any invention and skill

can keep poverty at arm's length by designing on wood for *Punch*, or *Judy*, or the *Illustrated News*, or the *Cornhill Magazine*, or *Good Words*, or one of that legion of periodicals, weekly and monthly, which bristle with clever woodcuts, and in which, as in an open tilting-yard, young squires of the pencil may win their spurs. Even when the power of invention is not present in a high degree there is much work of a prosaic kind required, in doing which a fair living may be obtained by a diligent young man of average ability, not to speak of the exceedingly valuable practice afforded by this kind of labour. It seems not unlikely that this field will enlarge. Society is meeting its modern abridgments of time for reading by a rational employment of the arts of illustration —the photograph and the wood-engraving. We learn in a glance nowadays more than our forefathers learned in a page of print ; yet if William Blake had lived in these days of ample opportunity his work would have been equally at a disadvantage. He dealt with the abiding, the abstract—with the eternal, and not the fleeting aspects of passing life. What the *Book of Job* is to the *Cornhill Magazine*, that was the mind of Blake to "the spirit of the age."

At fourteen he was apprenticed to Basire the engraver, by whom he was set to draw the monuments in Westminster Abbey and in the old churches about London — an occupation which had a great influence on his future manner of design. The influence of these solitary Gothic studies is traceable all through the future career of Blake. While the antique is the finest school for the study of the structure of the human form in its Adamic strength and beauty, the religious sculpture of the thirteenth and fourteenth centuries is the noblest material of study for the spiritual powers of form. The faces, though not often realising much delicacy of modelling, have far more expression than in the Greek statues. There is a mingling of ascetic severity with contemplative repose which transfuses itself into the beholder's mind, and gains upon him stealthily but surely, till he " forgets himself to marble." These monuments cannot be separated from the piles of wonderful architecture to which they belong. The niche in which a figure of bishop or king is placed is a portion of a great whole. It is usually adapted to its own position and lighting —a most important fact in monumental sculpture.

There is a fine passage in Rogers's *Italy*

describing the monument by Michael Angelo,
where a warrior sits musing in gigantic repose
under the shadow of his helmet, which casts so
deep a gloom over the upper part of the face that,
to the imagination of the beholder, the soul looks
out of the frowning shade, and, " like a basilisk, it
fascinates and is intolerable." A cast of the same
statue may be seen at the Crystal Palace, but
not with the same circumstantial advantages.
The ghostly fascination of that glooming shadow
is gone, though much remains.

The power which the statuary of one of our
old cathedrals may acquire over the mind is in-
conceivable, unless we do as Blake did during this
advantageous sojourn in the Abbey so replenished
with the most august memories and images. The
verger's voice must cease to echo among the
soaring shafts of the nave, the last vibration of
the organ must die among the groinings of the
roof. An absolute solitude must settle along the
marble tombs and into the shadowy recesses.
There must be no sounds but those faint, ceaseless, unearthly whispers of which every large
cathedral is full. Sighs, as it were, of the weary
centuries, more stilly and enchaining than utter
silence. Some definite object must be before us

to hold the mind above the airy fancies of such a loneliness ; some brass to be copied ; some Templar to sketch and measure in his chain-mail (which the younger Stothard etched so deliciously) as he lies stark along the dark time-gnawn marble, or crouching in the panel of a crumbling tomb ; or there must be archives to search, and worm-eaten parchments to unroll, among earthy odours. It is after months of such experience as this that we begin to realise the dreadful beauty, the high majesty, of Gothic shrines and their clinging soul of imagination—the soul of many, not of one—of the ages, not of years.

Mr. Gilchrist thinks it just possible that Blake may have seen the secret reopening of the coffin which revealed the face of Edward I. and the " yellow eyelids fallen " which dropped so sternly over his angry eyes at Carlisle. In Blake's angels and women, and, indeed, in most of his figures, we may see the abiding influence of these mediæval studies in that element of patriarchal quietude which sits meditating among the wildest storms of action.

The style of Basire laid the foundation of Blake's own practice as an engraver. It was dry and solid, and fitted for the realisation of strong and abstract pictorial thinking. While here he wrote many songs which were collected into a volume and published by the help of friends in 1783. In order to a right view of Blake's organisation, we must from the first bear in mind that he was a poetic thinker, who held in his hands two instruments of utterance. "With such a pencil, such a pen," few mortals were ever gifted. The combination of high literary power with high pictorial power is one of the rarest of endowments, and it is only among the loftiest order of minds—the Michael Angelos, the Leonardos, and the Raffaelles—that its presence is eminently distinguishable, though by them held in check.

The superb original strength of faculty to which the instrument is an accident, and which is able to work in any field, seems to be among Heaven's rarest gifts.

Of Blake's conditions and limitations as a general thinker, we shall have afterwards to speak. Thought with him leaned largely to the side of imagery rather than to the side of organised philosophy; and we shall have to be on our guard, while reading the record of his views and opinions, against the dogmatism which was more frequently based on exalted fancies than on the rock of abiding reason and truth. He never dreamed of questioning the correctness of his impressions. To him all thought came with the clearness and veracity of vision. The conceptive faculty, working with a perception of outward facts singularly narrow and imperfect, projected every idea boldly into the sphere of the actual. What he *thought*, he *saw*, to all intents and purposes; and it was this sudden and sharp crystallisation of inward notions into outward and visible signs which produced the impression on many beholders that reason was unseated—a surmise which his biographer regards so seriously as to devote a chapter to the consideration of the question, " Mad or not mad ? " If we say on this point at once that, without attempting definitions and distinctions, and while holding his substantial genius in the highest esteem, having long studied both his character and his works, we cannot but, on the whole, lean to the opinion that somewhere in the wonderful compound of flesh and spirit — somewhere in those recesses where the one runs into the other—he was " slightly touched," we shall save ourselves the necessity of attempting to defend certain phases of his work while maintaining an unqualified admiration for the mass and manner of his thoughts.

At the age of twenty-one he studied for a while in the recently-instituted Royal Academy, under the care of "Old Moser," whose fitness for his work may be judged by his recommendation to Blake to leave the study of the prints from Michael Angelo and Raffaelle, and to study those from Le Brun and Rubens. His reply to Moser gives us an insight into Blake's temper, and the strong combative modes of expression which, delivered, we are told, in quiet tones for the most part, characterised him through life: "How," says he, "did I secretly rage! I also spake my mind! I said to Moser, 'These things that you call finished are not even begun; how then can they be finished? The man who does not know the beginning cannot know the end of art.'"

The view he here took of pictorial appliances explains most of the theory which embraces his highest excellences and his greatest defects. The living model artificially *posed*, to his sensitive fancy, "smelt of mortality." "Practice and opportunity," he said, "very soon teach the language of art. Its spirit and poetry, centred in the imagination alone, never can be taught; and these make the artist." And again, a still more frank, and, to some minds, fatal confession, made in old age was this : " Natural objects *always did and do* weaken, deaden, and obliterate imagination in me." And yet, lest this should tend to lower the reader's interest in the faculty of the painter, let us indulge ourselves by quoting the motto selected by his biographer, to show the magnificent way in which he " lights his torch at Nature's funeral pile : "—

I ASSERT for myself that I do not behold the outward creation, and that to me it is hindrance, and not action. " What," it will be questioned, " when the sun rises do you not see a round disc of fire somewhat like a guinea ?" Oh no, no! I see an innumerable company of the heavenly host crying, " Holy, holy, holy is the Lord God Almighty !" I question not my corporeal eye any more than I would question a window concerning a sight. I look through it, and not with it.

One is reminded here of the more solemn adjudication of the relative claims of Mystery and Understanding given by St. Paul to the Corinthian Church. He does not deny the validity of the mystery yet expresses the strong views of a man of practical power. "I would rather speak five words with my understanding that I might teach others also than ten thousand words in an unknown tongue." We confess that we can never glance at the wild mysteries of *Thel*, and *Urizen*, and *Jerusalem*, without a frequent recurrence of this somewhat depreciatory phrase, "ten thousand words in an unknown tongue"; and, while acknowledging that, "howbeit in the spirit he speaketh mysteries," being strongly disposed to advance our sling-stone of "five" against the Goliath of "ten thousand." It seems to us also, that there is something misleading in the vague use of the words "practice and opportunity." The value of the old phrase "practice makes perfect" depends on what we mean by practice; as we take it, it means *the doing again and again the same kind of thing till we do it rightly;* and opportunity here is to be understood as *the presentation of appropriate and available means.*

Form, colour, light, and shade, and composition are the dictionary, the syntax, and the prosody of painting. The thought, the central idea of the picture, corresponds to its realisation, as thinking in words does to grammar. If dictionaries are of no use and grammar has no relation to thought,

then the details of the human or any other form
have no relation to painting. Indeed, to deny
this is to create a ridiculous paradox which one
may readily illustrate from the works of Blake
himself. What his inner eye may see in the
rising sun it is not for us to determine, but he
has drawn most pathetically in the drama of *Job*
both rising and descending suns. It is true that
he has not made them about the size of "a
guinea"; rather their arc spans the gloomy
horizon like a rainbow; but it is the segment of
a *circle*. Why did he not draw it square or
pyramidal? In order to draw at all he was
obliged to conform at least to *one* fact of nature,
and so far as he followed her at all she did not
"put him out," as Fuseli affirmed that nature did
for him likewise. The case in which he has
carried realistic idealism to its utmost verge is
perhaps in the strange design called *The Ghost
of a Flea;* but examine the features of the
ghost and say if for *material* he is not indebted
first to the baser and more truculent lines of the
human skull and nose and eye and hair, and
then to those insect-like elements which he had
observed in the plated beetle and the curious fly.

The solemn boundaries of form become ridiculous when they wander without enclosing some expressive fact visible to the eye either in heaven above or in earth beneath, and the question only remains, *How much* of this array of fact is needful adequately to convey *the given idea?* Jan Van Huysum would here pronounce a judgment entirely at the opposite pole from that of William Blake; and there is no surer mark of the true connoisseur than to be able to put himself *en rapport* with the designer, and to judge at once his aim and the degree in which it has been realised. It would introduce a dangerous axiom to say that, in proportion to the grandeur and unearthliness of a thought the aid of common facts is less needed; it entirely depends on *what* idea and *what* facts are in question. As applied to the human form, and to the highest idealisations of it yet known, and never to be surpassed, it would repay the reader who can see the collections of Michael Angelo's drawings at Oxford to observe with what grand reverence and timidity that learned pencil dwelt on the most minute expressions of detail from the crown of the head to the sole of the foot; and it was this abundant *learning* which enabled the far-stretching soul of the mighty Florentine to avoid and to eliminate amongst a

hundred details all those lines and forms which
would not accord with the brooding and colossal
majesty of his prophets, the frowning eagerness of
his sibyls, the cosmic strength of the first father,
or the waving beauty of the mother of us all.

A leading principle in Blake's design was that
" a good and firm outline " is its main requisite.
The claims of colour *versus* drawing are not very
fully opened out by his practice. Most of his
works were of a kind that singularly divided these
elements. Such of his productions as are most
delightful in colour are comparatively rude and
heavy in outline, and where his line is most sharp
and masterly, the element of colour is nearly or
altogether absent. His colour, again, was not so
much an imitative as a purely decorative agent.
The question as to whether the highest qualities of
colour are compatible with the highest qualities
of form seems to us to be not so much a matter
of abstract possibility as of actual and personal
practice. Tintoretto proposed to unite the " terrible
manner " and grand drawing of Michael Angelo
to the colour of Titian. There seems no reason
in the nature of these two elements why they
should not be united in the highest perfection.
Whether any genius will arise who will succeed

in doing this remains to be seen. Colour is to drawing what music is to rhythmic words. It is not under every set of conditions that music can be "married to immortal verse" with success. Much depends on the auditory, much on the apprehension of the musician. There are delights of the eye in colour alone which fully correspond to the delights of melody alone. We may see in so common an object as an old garden wall, and in the compass of a dozen moss-grown or lichen-stained bricks, with the irregular intervening mortar-lines, such hues and harmonies as will for a while give to the trained eye the same delight as a happy air of music gives to the instructed ear. No two red bricks are alike. Some deepen into rich and mottled purples, others kindle into ruddy orange, or subside into grays of the loveliest gradation. These accidental combinations of time-stain and emerald moss-growth, with the cloudy hues of the irregular brick-wall, are sufficient of themselves to satisfy an eye open to perceive and understand them.

In painting we may observe all manner of pleasant sophistries, which it is a fine holiday amusement to disentangle, arising from these subtle and indefinable relations of the pleasures of colour to the pleasures of form. How often we receive the most bewitching impressions from this sophistical play of the elements into each other, especially among the smaller and more sketchy examples of landscape art. Translate some of the sketches labelled "Evening," or "Solitude," into black and white and their glory would sink into a compost of rude forms, gloomy and incorrect, quite incapable of existing alone. Add the daring tints—the sombre greens, the purples, clouded with fluent ultramarine, the red bands of fire seen between dark tree stems, the amber seas of air, or "that green light which lingers in the West," and you are so far imposed upon that you do not dream of questioning the legality of the magic which, by its very intensification of mutual and interchangeable errors, produces on the mind the same sensation wrought on it when beholding the splendid shows of the landscape itself. We are far from believing that the rule and square of mere *literal* truth can be rigidly applied to human reproductions of nature. The difficulty of analysing the great equations and compensatory powers of art will ever make it an interesting subject of pursuit to the human race. It is a sea whose horizon fades—

For ever and for ever as we move.

K

Even when colour is used in the engraver's
sense of black and white alone, these com-
minglings as mystic as twilight retain their power
over the eye and fancy.  Opposite to page 270,
vol. i. of Blake's *Life*, there are three woodcuts
which fully illustrate our meaning.  They were
done to ornament the *Pastorals* of Virgil, edited
by Dr. Thornton, and are of a degree of rudeness
apparently verging on incapacity.  Yet we would
venture to ask any competent judge whether an
effect in a high degree poetic is not produced by
the total sentiment of the design.  To our eye
they seem to contain 'a germ of that grandeur and
sense of awe and power of landscape which in
some of his works John Linnell has carried out
so finely, where dawn-lights dream over tranquil
folds or evening slowly leaves the valley flock to
the peace of night.

In confirmation of our views we will quote
from Mr. Gilchrist.  The signal agreement of men
so well qualified to judge as those named in the
extract is worth notice :—

The rough unconventional work of a mere prentice
hand to the art of wood-engraving, they are in effect
vigorous and artist-like, recalling the doings of Albert
Dürer and the early masters whose aim was to give

ideas, not pretty language. When he sent in these seventeen, the publishers, unused to so daring a style, were taken aback and declared "this man must do no more"; nay, were for having all he had done re-cut by one of their regular hands. The very engravers received them with derision, crying out in the words of the critic, "This will never do." Blake's merits, seldom wholly hidden from his artist-contemporaries, were always impenetrably dark to the book and print selling genus. Dr. Thornton had in his various undertakings been munificent to artists to an extent which brought him to poverty. But he had himself no knowledge of art, and despite kind intentions, was disposed to take his publishers' views. However, it fortunately happened that meeting one day several artists at Mr. Aders's table—Lawrence, James Ward, Linnell, and others—conversation fell on the Virgil. All present expressed warm admiration of Blake's art, and *of those designs and woodcuts in particular.* By such competent authority reassured, if also puzzled, the good Doctor began to think there must be more in them than he and his publishers could discern. The contemplated sacrifice of the blocks already cut was averted.

And so we have these three grand but uncouth designs still preserved to us, in one of which the shepherd is eloquent among the ewes and sucking lambs, another where a traveller walks solemnly

on among the hills alone, while in a third " the
young moon with the old moon in her arms "
rises over fallen ranks of wheat. Thought cannot
fathom the secret of their power, and yet the
power is there.

Blake's reverence for " a firm and determinate
outline" misled him chiefly where his works are
intended to be elaborately shaded. The importance of right outline to all noble drawing cannot
be overestimated. It must never be forgotten,
however, that outline only represents the surface
of objects in their extreme confines right and left,
above and below, nor that the eye recognises the
intermediate spaces, with all their projection and
depression as clearly as it sees the limit which is
called outline.

To take a simple illustration of this. The outline of an egg, with its lovely tapering lines, is
primarily needful to record the image of an egg
on paper or canvas. If Flaxman draws the egg
from which Castor and Pollux issued, the oval
boundary is sufficient. It is accepted as a type of
the egg just as the flat figures of his designs from
Homer or Hesiod are accepted as the types of
men. But the case is altered if the relief of the
whole has to be given by shading. An egg all

outline in the midst of a shaded design would look as flat as a small oval kite. To produce its proportion of resemblance, the outline must be filled with its pale moonshine gradations up to the central high light, by means of which the surface appears to swell forward to the eye. These gradations and shaded forms must be in their true place as much as the bounding line, or it will not yield the correct impression. If we apply this rule to each single feature of the human face and figure we shall see that while the firm and decided outline must be given correctly, it is only a hundredth part of the truth. Each point of the surface of the body if turned sufficiently would *become* outline, and indeed there is no portion of the exposed superficies which may not be called outline in this sense. It is owing to a one-sided view of the question of drawing such forms that we have to search among the often uncouth and broken shading in the plates of Blake for that powerful and accurate outline which we are sure almost universally to find.

After these fair, nay ample opportunities for learning the appliances of design, Blake began to invent the long series of drawings, semi-paintings, and etchings, on which, together with a large section of his lyrics, his solid fame must ever rest. He supported himself by journeyman's work for the publishers. In 1780 he exhibited a drawing of "The Death of Earl Godwin," at the Royal Academy, and continued for years occasionally to exhibit there.

All his works were done in pencil or in water-colours. "With the still tougher mechanical difficulties of oil-painting he never fairly grappled," and, indeed, with his views of the inadequacy and unimportance of the solid facts of nature, it was utterly impossible that he should ever have been able to use with effect such an ample vehicle of expression. He married, and his marriage forms a pretty story, told in Allan Cunningham's sketch as well as more at length here. His wife became the faithful "Kate," whose image is inextricably bound up with that of the old man who attained "to something like prophetic strain," in the ears of the small band of faithful young disciples, some of whom survive to this day.

Catherine Boucher was endowed with a loving, loyal nature, an adaptive open mind, capable of profiting by good teaching, and of enabling her, under constant high influence, to become a meet companion to her imaginative husband in his solitary and wayward course. Uncomplainingly and helpfully she shared the low and rugged fortunes which over-originality ensured as his unvarying lot in life. She had mind and the ambition which follows. Not only did she prove a good housewife on straitened means, but in after years, under his tuition and hourly companionship, she acquired, besides the useful arts of reading and writing, that which very few uneducated women with the honestest effort can succeed in attaining, some footing of equality with her husband. She in time came to work off his engravings, as though she had been bred to the trade ; nay, imbibed enough of his very spirit to reflect it in design which might almost have been his own.

It was a fortunate circumstance for Blake in a professional sense that he had no children. In many cases the necessities of a family rouse and develop the resources of the parent mind and discover means of support where none appeared. This would have been impossible with such a nature as Blake's. He might have drudged and slaved at prosaic work with the graver and so have been prevented from finding his own sphere as an inventor, but he could not have made his works a whit more acceptable to the general taste. He needed no spur ; his powers were

always awake, always on the stretch ; and we
have probably from his hand all that could ever
have been obtained under the most favourable
circumstances.    Many a man is depressed by
poverty and anxiety to a level below that of his
secret capacities.    It was not so here.    The last
touches of his steady graving tool are as cool and
strong in the latest of his works as in the earliest.
It was not in the power of neglect or pain or sick-
ness or age or infirmity to quench a vital force so
native and so fervent.

He and his wife took a little house in Green
Street, Leicester-fields.    He had become acquainted
with Flaxman the sculptor, and was by him introduced to " the celebrated Mrs. Matthew," of whom
the oblivious waves of time have left no authentic
trace, except that she loved letters and art and
held elegant *conversaziones*, at which Blake used to
appear, and where he used to recite or sing his
sweet lyrical ballads with music composed also
by himself, to, probably, Mrs. Chapone, Mrs.
Barbauld, Mrs. Brooke, Mrs. Carter, or Mrs.
Montague.    In these light airy associations " he
was listened to by the company with profound
silence, and allowed by most of the visitors to
possess original and extraordinary merit."    " His

unbending deportment, or what his adherents are
pleased to call his manly firmness of opinion,
which certainly was not at all times considered
pleasing by every one," was the probable cause
of the cessation of his visits to these and to the
like assemblies. The commerce of true genius
with the genius of "respectability" seldom ends
with entire satisfaction to both parties. Their
current coin of interchange does not consist of
measurable equivalents, the accounts at length
become confused and the books are closed.

He engraved from Stothard and others for the
magazines, mortified sometimes to see that his
own designs had been the foundation, so he said,
of the subject he engraved; indeed, Fuseli himself acknowledged that "Blake was good to steal
from." We may understand the force of this
saying if we only look at a design of early date
by Blake, called "Plague," well known by means
of frequent reproductions. An inexorable severe
grandeur pervades the general lines; an inexplicable woe hangs over it, as of Samaria in the deadly
siege when Joram, wandering on the walls, was
obliged to listen to the appeal of the cannibal
mother; a sense of tragic culmination, the stroke
of doom irreversible, comes through the windows of

the eyes as they take in the straight black lines
of the pall and bier, the mother falling from her
husband's embrace with her dying child, one fair
corpse scarcely earthed over in the foreground, and
the black funereal reek of a distant fire which
consumes we know not what unseen horror.  It
is enough to excite the imagination of the greatest
historical painter.   And yet the manner is so dry,
so common, even so uninteresting, and so unlikely
to find its way to " every drawing-room table," that
a man of accomplishments and appreciative powers,
but without the "vision and the faculty divine,"
would be sorely tempted to convey the thinking to
his own canvas, and array it in forms more attractive to the taste, without being haunted by the
fear that his theft would be speedily recognised.

In 1784 he set up a print shop at 27 Broad
Street, near where he was born, and pursued his
work as an engraver in partnership with a fellow-
pupil at Basire's.   Mrs. Blake "helped in the
shop " while he wrought at the desk.   The partnership came to nothing.   He removed to Poland
Street and continued as before inventing poems
and designs and writing enthusiastic or sharp
comments in the margins of his favourite books,
Lavater and others.   We may form a conception

of his daily attitude if we peep into the plain little room with the frame of tissue paper inclining over his desk to moderate the light on his copper-plate, a thumbed "Lavater" by his side, in which he now and then writes a tender or pugnacious comment.

When he was a little over thirty years of age he collected and published one of his sweetest and most original works, *The Songs of Innocence*, en-graving the poem in a singular way with delightful designs on copper. The plaques upon which these designs were made still exist. They are somewhat like rude, deep-cut casts from engraved wood blocks. They were drawn on the copper with some thick liquid impervious to acid; the plate was then immersed in aquafortis and "bitten" away, so that the design remained in relief. These he printed with his own hand in various tones of brown, blue, and gray, tinting them afterwards by hand into a sort of rainbow-coloured, innocent page, in which the thrilling music of the verse and the gentle bedazzlement of the lines and colours so intermingle that the mind hangs in a pleasant uncertainty as to whether it is a picture that is singing or a song which has newly budded and blossomed into colour and

form.   All is what the title imports ; and though
they have been of late years frequently quoted
and lose half their sweetness away from the
embowering leaves and tendrils which clasp them,
running gaily in and out among the lines, we
cannot but gratify ourselves and our readers with
one light peal of the fairy bells :—

> Sweet dreams form a shade
> O'er my lovely infant's head,
> Sweet dreams of pleasant streams,
> By happy, silent, moony beams.
>
> Sweet sleep, with soft down
> Weave thy brows an infant crown ;
> Sweet sleep, angel mild,
> Hover o'er my happy child.
>
> Sweet smiles in the night,
> Hover over my delight ;
> Sweet smiles, mother's smiles,
> All the livelong night beguiles.
>
> Sweet moans, dovelike sighs,
> Chase not slumber from thy eyes,
> Sweet moans, sweeter smiles,
> All thy dovelike moans beguiles.
>
> Sleep, sleep, happy child,
> All creation slept and smiled ;
> Sleep, sleep, happy sleep,
> While o'er thee thy mother weep.
>
> Sweet babe, in thy face
> Holy image I can trace ;
> Sweet babe, once like thee,
> Thy Maker lay and wept for me.

This is the tone of them; and there are many
such strains as these that deserve to be much
better known than they are, notwithstanding the
bad grammar that mingles with their innocent
music.    There is a serene unconsciousness of
arbitrary human law in genius such as this; it
floats with the lark in a "privacy of glorious
light" where the grammatical hum of the critics
cannot disturb its repose.   We are reminded of
the startling question of the Yorkshire orator
when repudiating the bonds of syntax and pro-
nunciation, " *Who invented grammar I should like
to know?*   I've as much right to invent grammar
as any of them!"   Whatever we might concede
to the Yorkshire orator, we may readily agree not
to be inexorably severe in the application of our
canons to the productions of such a genius as that
of Blake.

Amongst Blake's designs there is one which
affects the eye wonderfully, where huge inter-
twisted trunks writhe up one side of the page,
while on the other springs, apparently, Jack's
immortal laddered bean-stalk, aiming at heaven;
between the two on the blank white sky hang
mystical verses, and below is a little vision of
millennial rest; naked children sport with the

lion and ride the lioness in playful domination while secure humanity sleeps at ease among them.

Yet Blake had a difficult and repulsive phase in his character. It seems a pity that men so amiable and tender, so attractive to one's desire for fellowship, should prove on close contact to have a side of their nature so adamantine and full of self-assertion and resistance that they are driven at last to dwell in the small circle of friends who have the forbearance to excuse their peculiarities and the wit to interpret their moods and minds :—

> Nor is it possible to thought
> A greater than itself to know.

In this sphinx-like and musical couplet, Blake himself hits the true basis of the reason why men whose genius is at once so sweet, so strong, and so unusual are largely overlooked during life, and are difficult of exposition when the fluctuations and caprices of life no longer interfere to prevent a fair estimate of their powers and performances.

After these exquisite poems, which come nearest to the universal heart, Blake struck off on his own strange wings into regions where we will not

attempt to follow him.  Those who wish to see
what may be said for the scope and design of the
series of Blake's illustrated mysteries may consult
Mr. Swinburne's inquiries into and eloquent comments on them.  For our own part, their chief
value seems to consist in the fragments of astonishing pictorial invention which they contain, hints
and indications of which are given in facsimile
in Mr. Gilchrist's well illustrated *Life*.  There can
be no question that the first impression produced
by them is, that they are the production of a mad-
man of superb genius ; and this impression is so
strong that few people would be persuaded to do
more than glance at what would confirm their
judgment.  Here is one of those firm questions
which the man whose mind is unbalanced will
ask with unflinching eye—he is talking familiarly
to Isaiah : " Does a firm persuasion that a thing is
so, make it so ? "  What an entangling preliminary
question before he ventures to slip the leash of
some " subjective " horror !  " I was in a printing-
house in hell."  What a *nonchalant*, passing introduction to a subject !  " My friend the angel
climbed up from his station into the mill " ; here
is the easy way in which he treats principalities
and powers.  " So the angel said, ' Thy phantasy

has imposed upon me, and thou oughtest to be ashamed.' I answered, 'We *impose on one another*, and it is but lost time to converse with you, whose works are only analytics.'" Here is a man, not exactly a fool, who "rushes in where angels fear to tread," and snaps his fingers in their faces. There is no wonder if ordinary civilians found such a one to be difficult to get on with.

And yet an unconquerable indifference to his transcendental philosophy does not in the least interfere with our veneration of the artist, as such. We hold that the "creative" and the "critical" faculties are seldom found in close and powerful alliance, and that often in proportion to the intensity and energy of the former is the dormancy, if not the incapacity of the latter. In the procession of his own labours the artist unconsciously selects or rejects. He is conscious that deep down in the laws of thought his justification is to be found, but he has neither time nor inclination to become a pearl diver, when the riches of the

> Eternal deep,
> Haunted for ever by the Eternal mind,

come and pour themselves unsought at his feet. A life of analysis and reconstruction he leaves to

others, and he is the happiest painter or singer
who leaves the philosophies

On Argive heights divinely sung,

to the Argives ; that is to say, so far as any
practical intermeddling with them is concerned.
Even if he be capable of entering the region he
acts most wisely who follows Mr. Ruskin's short
advice to a painter, "Fit yourself for the best
company and—*keep out of it.*"

As to any serious consideration of Blake's
vocation to teach aught of morals, of theology, or
non-theology, of Christian Atheism, or Atheistic
Christianity; we, with "the volume of the Book,"
which "is written," in our hands—"calmly, but
firmly, and finally," on a general glance at the
tone and tenor of these portentous scrolls of
*Thel* and *Urizen*, these *Marriages of Heaven
and Hell*, which would look blasphemous if we
did not tenderly recollect by whom they were
written, refuse any serious further investigation
of their claims, and must dismiss them, not scorn-
fully though it may be sorrowfully.  We regard
them rather as we regard the gentle or exalted
incoherences of a dear friend's delirium, for our
theory of the mental structure of Blake renders

them as harmless to us as his gentle *Songs of Innocence*, but on this ground we dismiss them— repeating the words before applied to them, only with no anger or disdain—that they are " *Ten thousand words in an unknown tongue.*"

But not shelving or ignoring the illuminated pages themselves, their inventive power remains, and they may be regarded as a repository of winged and fiery imagery which will be useful to us in our attempts to realise things invisible in so far as the elements of matter may bridge over for our conceptive faculties the gulfs between the seen and unseen, and in so far as they may be made to illustrate phases of thought to which they were not in the first instance intended to apply. Many of his less elaborated designs are eminently suggestive in this direction, and may be referred to in the woodcuts. Take them one by one, suppose no further relation than each has to its significant title, and we are wholly satisfied. We will not say how often and with what fine effect one of these rude but noble squares enters before the inner eye and allies itself with the current stream of thought.

" *Alas !* "—that is the simple title of one of them, a boy chasing winged loves which he kills

with his catching; need we move farther to seek
our goal of meaning? " *What is Man?* "  That
caterpillar, huge and spectral, crawling over the
oak leaf under which the baby-faced chrysalis
lies expecting its life and its wings — to be
" crushed before the moth " in due time.  Can we
not find our own sufficient application of such a
wondrous image?  " *I want! I want!* "  Here is
" the globe's last verge " which both Dryden and
Blake contrived (but with very different faculties
and success) to see ; where, according to Dryden,
we may behold " the ocean leaning on the sky."
Here Blake, on this hint, boldly heaves his ladder
to the hollow bosom of " our rolling neighbour," the
crescent moon, and begins to climb fearless as
Blondin, and cross the star-sown abyss to satisfy
his " want."  So with each of these precious little
bald and grand designs, the last of which is almost
appalling.  A white, unearthly figure with a wand
—a figure neither large nor small, for it is of no
size to the judgment and imagination—cowers and
stares beneath the root of a forest oak, a huge
worm winds round before her feet, and the in-
scription is, " *I have said to the worm, Thou art my
mother and my sister.* "  Surely any one who ever
sat awestruck over the *Book of Job* and heard

the "deep sad music of humanity" coming on the long-drawn gust of Time from those lands of Uz, would feel that here was one worthy and sufficient interpretation of the idea of the verse and of those other kindred upbreathings from the grave and wailings of the haunted "house appointed for all living," of which the early chapters of the *Book of Job* are full.

Laying aside these works as philosophies or preachings and returning upon them as strange pictures intended for the informing of the imagination through the eye, it is impossible to put into words the delight and restless wonder they excite. Without referring to the large collection of Blake's drawings which we remember having the privilege of being shown to us by Mr. Gilchrist while writing his book (a treat never to be forgotten, for the various possessors of his books and designs, among whom Lord Houghton was one of the most appreciative owners of curious specimens, had furnished him with a sufficient mass of materials), we will rather call attention to such as may be accessible to every reader of the *Biography*. We invite the reader to turn to one of them, and to the opposite page, which is a facsimile of one of Blake's leaves from *America*, reduced —but by an unerring "photo-lithographic" process

—to half the size, and printed as nearly as possible in the colour used as a groundwork for his hand-tinting, so that we are looking, in fact, at an autograph. Study carefully the design on the upper part of the left-hand page. By a sheer breadth of black, sharply contrasted with the white page by some inexplicable magic, there is conveyed the impression of a space in the upper skies, where —coming we know and care not whence and hasting we know not whither—is a wild swan bridled and mounted by an elf into whose history and significance we shall never trouble ourselves to inquire. But we appeal to the intelligent observer whether that design does not kindle the page into a silver light and hasten the spirits into a breezy swiftness of enjoyment and strike the harp of memory within him, perhaps making him recall the fine image in the *Palace of Art*—

> Far as the wild swan wings to where the sky
> Dipt down to sea and sands.

It is in this, as in ten thousand other ways, that the pencil becomes the gorgeous sister and handmaiden of the poet's pen, kindling into inciting suggestion his flying images and doubling the value of his priceless words. The eye is irresistibly

drawn below to the bottom of the page; and what
a rich and rare sense of visual joy comes as we
see that serpent-"dragon of the prime," coming
carelessly from nowhere and going by shining
cloud and crescent and sparkling star into the
emptiness of night, his tail curled, against all
nature, into a writing-master's flourish, his sole
apparent object being to oblige three merry fairies
with a morning ride!   We pray you look at his
eye and mouth!   How he enjoys the fun, and
what a large reserve of cunning meaning there
is all over his corrugated face as he puts out his
forked tongue, most probably at the metaphy-
sicians, or, however ungratefully, at Blake's manu-
script itself.

Turn to the right-hand page from *America;*
its relations to the great Republic seem remote to
the sense.   Yet in the "tall talk" in the "centre"
of the design, the strong and terribly bloodshot
tone of which is greatly subdued by the pretty
little twirls and twiddles into which its letters
run, we see a foreshadowing of at least an *accusation* against *America*—and in the capacity of
the genii who weigh all creation in their own
scales and fly away with the sword of the earth
and fling world-powers into the void as easily as

Athamas dashed Learchus in pieces, and who
perform Blondin feats on "Serpents of Eternity,"
instead of tight-ropes, between spires of rushing
flame ascending out of the abyss, we see allusions
closer than we might at first suppose to the
"greatest people on the face of the earth." Yet
their chief value does not lie in this. It is in the
mysterious fascination of line, the mingling of
creative might and childlike play, the astonishing
power which by dark and strongly imprinted
curves can give—"*lucus a non lucendo*"—the
sense of flashing flame, the power to "make black
seem white," which so enchains and half stupefies
the fancy. As a specific example of this, look at
what we may call the prophecy of Blondin, the
Herculean tumbler on the Serpent of Eternity.
How amazingly grand the lines! Carve it in
onyx, and have we not an antique gem of the
finest character, Phidias and Michael Angelo in
little? Yet pass below the giant acrobat's elbow
and Michael Angelo subsides into a schoolboy
finishing his little theme with an innocent flourish.
This is Blake all over: now he is a Titan hurling
rocks at the gods, now a chubby boy toddling to
the infant-school and singing his pretty echoing
song.

Beside these books and "prophecies," Blake
made many designs of a separate or serial kind,
and found in Mr. Butts a kind, steadfast, and
appreciative patron. A large collection of these
works is still in the possession of his son, Captain
Butts. For nearly thirty years the modest, simple-
living Blake found a constant resource in this
worthy friend's patronage. It is a beautiful
picture of his typical life of Arcadian simplicity
and sufficiency to see this plain liver and high
thinker taking his weekly design to sell for a
very moderate price and returning to dream and
draw and engrave in his own humble home.

Out of this simple life issued in 1794 the *Songs
of Experience*. Flaxman used to exclaim, " Sir,
his poems are as grand as his pictures"; and
Wordsworth " read them with delight." Yet words
do not tell the half of Blake's poems—do not
reveal half the man. Some pieces will bear
separation from the rainbow pages on which they
originally appeared ; others, and most of them,
lose half their thrill and motion when enchained
in the printer's " forme." When the brown poem
and rough ground-lines of the design were stamped
on the rough paper by the rude press, then his
lyrical fingers playing with the prisms of water-

colour washed and touched all over them in a
way not to be described — poem and picture
twined fondly round each other in a bath of
colour and light refusing to be separated. So
that he who is to understand Blake must be
admitted to the penetralia where such sights are
to be seen. Not that he had any special aim at
exceptional seclusion. "Come in," he would say;
"it is only Adam and Eve," as in an anecdote
narrated at length by Mr. Gilchrist which adds
another proof of our theory that a veil of innocent
unreason spread its haze over one side of his nature.
Surely by this time the little poem which begins—

> Tiger, tiger, burning bright
> In the forests of the night,

and which Charles Lamb called "glorious," is
pretty well known, as also the song beginning—

> Piping down the valleys wild.

The exceeding delicacy and sweetness of some
separate verses in his poems convey that sense of
enchantment which Scott describes as coming over
him at any recurrence of the stanza—

> The dews of summer night did fall,
>   The moon, sweet regent of the sky,
> Silvered the walls of Cumnor Hall,
>   And many an oak that grew thereby.

It is hard to say in what this happy quality consists. To our own mind there is something of it
in a song of Bulwer, in the *Last Days of Pompeii*,
beginning—

> By the cool banks where soft Cephisus flows,
> A voice sailed trembling down the waves of air.

To which Blake's *Song to the Muses* might have
given the keynote—

> Whether on Ida's shady brow
>    Or in the chambers of the East,
> The chambers of the sun that now
>    From ancient melody have ceased.
>
> Whether in heaven ye wander fair,
>    Or the green corners of the earth,
> Or the blue regions of the air,
>    Where the melodious winds have birth.
>
> Whether on crystal rocks ye rove,
>    Beneath the bosom of the sea,
> Wandering in many a coral grove,
>    Fair Nine, forsaking poesy.
>
> How have you left your ancient love,
>    The bards of old enjoyed in you?
> The languid strings do scarcely move,
>    The sound is forced, the notes are few.

There is this ineffable charm of scenery and
sound in these lines from *Night*—

Farewell, green fields, and happy grove,
  Where flocks have ta'en delight,
Where lambs have nibbled, silent move
  The feet of angels bright.
    Unseen they pour blessing,
    And joy without ceasing,
    On each bud and blossom,
    And each sleeping bosom.

They look in every thoughtless nest
  Where birds are covered warm,
They visit caves of every beast,
  To keep them all from harm.
    If they see any weeping
    That should have been sleeping,
    They pour sleep on their head,
    And sit down by the bed.

The same simple and tender mood of soul that originated such child-melodies as "Gentle Jesus, meek and mild," which brings tears down the cheeks of the ruggedest sailor, and has touched the secret fount of tears in many an unconfessing heart, handled this "rural pen," and "stained that water clear," and wrote that happy song—

Every child shall joy to hear.

To such influences grown men also do well to keep open their souls; for Blake, in his *Auguries of Innocence*, writes—

He who mocks the infant's faith
Shall be mocked in age and death.

There is so much pleasure in copying out some of
these fragments, that we are tempted to linger a
little longer over them.   The silver Shakespearean
song of "Take, oh take those lips away!" has
always sounded like a honey-laden breeze of
Hymettus.  There is the same nameless spell
in these words of Blake rolled sweetly on each
other, as the rose-leaves curl towards the heart of
the rose—

> Never seek to tell thy love,
>   Love that never told can be,
> For the gentle wind doth move
>   Silently, invisibly.

Here are two stanzas, not so remarkable for their
pure melody but containing a wonderfully felici-
tous image—

> Mock on, mock on, Voltaire, Rousseau !
>   Mock on, mock on, 'tis all in vain !
> You throw the sand against the wind,
>   And the wind blows it back again.
>
> And every sand becomes a gem,
>   Reflected in the beams divine ;
> Blown back, they blind the mocking eye,
>   But still in Israel's paths they shine.

In a motto prefixed to the *Auguries of Innocence,* he expresses that power which is given
to genuine imagination and which so distinctively
separates it from the rest of the faculties, or

rather, enables it both to use and master and
transcend them all—the power

> To see a world in a grain of sand,
>   And a heaven in a wild flower,
> Hold infinity in the palm of your hand
>   And eternity in an hour.

Thus we are led on by their alluring sweetness as
we are led from bush to bush by the piping of a
bird of unusual note and brilliant plume.

But our material swells beyond expectation
and we must return to his history.   He illustrated
Young's *Night Thoughts* for Edwards of New Bond
Street, doing forty-three plates in one year, which
seems to us a wonderful testimony to his diligence
and skill.   These designs, however, were not
among his most successful works.   The most
remarkable episode in his career is the four
years' residence at Felpham, near Bognor, on the
coast of Sussex.   He was forty-three years old
when it commenced, and the occasion of it was
that Hayley, the poet of the *Triumphs of Temper*
and the friend of Cowper and Romney, desired
him to illustrate his *Life of Cowper* then under
way.   Here he resided in a cottage, which we
visited with reverence not very long since—a
cottage by the sea, within sight of its waters and

sound of its everlasting roll. On the shore, at the
end of a little lane leading thitherward, he often
paced in the twilight, his friends and chance
acquaintance in these rambles being "Moses and
the Prophets, Homer, Dante, and Milton—all
majestic shadows, gray but luminous and superior
to the common height of men." Blake was a
little under the "common height of men," and it
would have been a notable sight to have passed
by him or seen him in the distance, walking the
brown sands in the dusky air, and conversing on
easy terms with these stately shades.

He was recalled to the "visible diurnal sphere"
rather rudely during his sojourn by the sea by no
less an incident than that of being tried for high
treason! How a man so harmless and hermit-
like came to find himself in such an astonishing
position may well excite the reader's inquiry. It
happened in this way—

One day in August a drunken soldier—probably
from the barracks at Aldwick or Chichester—broke
into the little slip of garden fronting the painter's
sequestered cottage, and was there as violent and un-
ruly as is the wont of drunken soldiers to be. He
refused to go. The red-coat was a great hulking
fellow, the artist of short stature, but robust, well-

knit, with plenty of courage and capable of a
supernatural energy, as it were, on occasions. In
his exasperation he laid hold of the intrusive black-
guard and turned him out neck and crop in a kind of
inspired frenzy, which took the man aback and fairly
frightened him ; such volcanic wrath being a novelty
in his experience. "I do not know *how* I did it, but
I did it," said Blake afterwards, and was himself disposed to attribute his success to that demoniac or
spiritual *will* by stress of which he believed a man
might achieve anything physical. In the course of
the scuffle, while blows were being exchanged, angry
words passed of course—the red-coated bully vapour-
ing that "he was the king's soldier," and so forth. . . .
[In fact, Blake swore at king and soldier.] The
soldier, bent on revenge, out of Blake's hasty words
made up a story and got a comrade to bear him out,
that his rough host had been guilty of seditious language. The sequel forcibly reminds us we are here
in the times of "the good old king," not in those of Vic-
toria. The soldier and "his mate" made their charge
on oath before a magistrate, and Blake had to stand
his trial for high treason at the next quarter sessions.

By Hayley's efforts and the skill of Samuel
Rose, his counsel, whose name occurs in *Cowper's
Correspondence,* he was acquitted.

Mrs. Blake used afterwards to tell how in the
middle of the trial, when the soldier invented some-

thing to support his case, her husband called out
"*False !*" with characteristic vehemence, and in a tone
which electrified the whole court and carried conviction with it.   Rose greatly exerted himself for the
defence.   In his cross-examination of the accuser, he
"most happily exposed," says Hayley, "the falsehood
and malignity of the charge, and also spoke very
eloquently for his client," though in the midst of his
speech seized with illness and concluding it with
difficulty.    Blake's   neighbours   joined   Hayley   in
giving him the same character of habitual gentleness
and peaceableness, which must have a little astonished
the soldier after his peculiar experience of those
qualities.   "After a long and very patient hearing,"
the *Sussex Advertiser* continues, "he was by the jury
acquitted, which so gratified the auditory that the
court was in defiance of all decency thrown into up-
roar by their noisy exultations.   During the sessions
the Duke of Richmond sat the first day from ten in
the morning till eight at night without quitting the
court or taking any refreshment."

The account of his work here and his agree-
ments and disagreements with the only partially
appreciative Hayley is very delightful ; and the
cottage, with its "thatched roof of rusty gold,"
will always form a lovely element in the "study
of imagination" which any one loving Blake and

his works will frequently revolve.   One comment
from Hayley's pen is worth extracting here as
throwing light on the characteristics of Blake's
life and mind.   "Engraving," he writes, "of all
human works appears to require the largest
portion of patience, and he happily possesses
more of that inestimable virtue than ever I saw
united before to an imagination so lively and so
prolific."   Having hinted our own doubts as to
the absolute saneness of his whole mind, we are
anxious to set before that of the reader an
accurate outline of the developments of his life
in daily habit and practice.   Let us dismiss any,
the least, image of a dangerous or lunatic mental
error.   A patient, plodding, regular, daily course
of strenuous employment severe and distinct, with
intervals of quiet, unobtrusive meditation and
converse flashing now and then with spirit, but
usually mild and calm, saying his wild sayings
in a way totally unalarming—this is the image
which the biographer and one or two who have
known him have impressed on our own understanding and memory,—a man sweet and charming
among the young and those who were earnest
in the pursuit of truth, but like William the
Conqueror, being " stronger than his foregangers,"

M

he was stern to those who opposed his views or
thwarted his will—yet speaking in a low and
musical voice with a gentle enthusiasm and a
natural high-pitched politeness, the fruit of
reverence and love.

Hayley endeavoured to persuade Blake to
undertake the painting of miniature portraits
while at Felpham, and introduced him to Lord
Egremont of Petworth, Lord Bathurst of Havant,
Mrs. Poole, and others, and obtained him commissions, thinking that this work might promote
the painter's fortunes. It was a good thought of
Hayley's, and in almost any other case might
have proved the making of Blake in those days.
Those days are, alas, no more. The photograph
has demolished the old-fashioned delightful miniature. The mournful "turn-out" of the profession
one by one into fresh fields and new labours, as
the foundations of their occupation were gradually
crumbling under their feet, forms one of the most
interesting episodes in the history of modern art.
Some retired on their well-earned savings to the
quiet occasional exercise of their pencil ; the
larger number were absorbed in the photographic
"studio," as it is euphemistically called, and found
a more profitable if less meritorious sphere of

action. The older men who had not "made hay
while the sun shone," and yet were paralysed, as
it were, by the "sunstroke," retired to comparative
indigence and neglect. But in the beginning of
the century an ordinary skilful hand might gain
plenty of money by the miniature, which was in
constant demand among persons of any means or
station. The practice, too, of portraiture is one
most useful and favourable to the painter of works
of imagination where the human figure is employed.

Leslie has some valuable remarks on this subject in his *Handbook for Young Painters*. He
points out the great advantage which accrues to a
student from having a constant series of models,
who not only sit to him while he masters the
millionfold details of texture, drawing, expression,
colour, and handling, but who pay him well for
his self-given lessons, and are as a rule not difficult to please if his temper be easy and his
behaviour courteous. How many a painter of
middle age will recall those days before the flood
of photography, when his pleasant sitters came
duly from day to day, or when he was received
with welcome into the country house to paint the
inmates and make a new circle of lifelong friends !

He will sigh as he thinks how far removed and how unlikely speedily to return those days of pleasure and profit are. But though Blake might have greatly gained both as to knowledge and purse by such practice as miniature painting would have afforded, his original structure here appears vindicating itself as usual. No prospect of gain could turn him aside from the flinty mountain path on which so early he had set his feet, and which he continued to climb till he reached its summit. He studied Greek with Hayley and had a good capacity for languages. He learned French so as to be able to read it in the compass of a few weeks; and at sixty years of age he studied Italian in order to read Dante. "The kind indefatigable Blake—our alert Blake" —for a while seems to have enjoyed his retreat by the sea.

Hayley appears to have been full of kind intentions, but he had not the faculty really to understand or appreciate his guest and fellow-labourer. He was not without sensibility and taste, but he was fussy, flighty, and shallow. His wit was of the small and twittering sort, as the note of a sparrow to the prolonged and varied moonlight song of Philomel, and his sentiment

was of the kind we call lackadaisical, the mere
lady's-maid of the muse with "watery eyne." The
oak-like strength and harebell tenderness of the
painter could not very long live in such a
smothering atmosphere, and an end was put to
their intercourse. Hayley's society became irk-
some and his sentiments distasteful to Blake, and,
as his manner was, he flung satirical couplets off
against him into a little volume, now in the hands
of Mr. D. G. Rossetti—to such effect as this—

> Thy friendship oft hath made my heart to ache ;
> Do be my enemy, for friendship's sake.

He returned to London, to South Molton
Street, near Oxford Street, and resumed his
"Prophetic" works, illustrated with the "giant
forms," as usual—*Jerusalem* and *Milton*, etc.
On these followed an edition of Blair's *Grave*, in
which the designs were made by Blake and the
etching done in a very first-rate way by Schiavonetti. We well remember the thrill of wonder and
delight with which we found this volume in a
public library in the country in the days of youth.
The complexities of the occasion, the treatment of
Blake by Cromek, and Blake's own indignation, we
will indicate at some length.

Blake was near fifty years of age and in the

zenith of his strength when he was recommended
to the public by Mr. Malkin, headmaster of Bury
Grammar School, who published a highly-curious
volume of memoirs of his son who died in his
seventeenth year, and whose precocity of intellect
was something appalling.  The intellectual sentiment of the time was unfavourable to the right
guidance of such a mind.  We catch a glimpse of
it in the memoirs of Mrs. Schimmelpenninck.
The style of ordinary composition suffered from
the heavy rolling reverberation of the Johnsonian
dialect and the detestable classicisms of the French
Revolution.  Every well-educated mother was
Cornelia or the mother of the Gracchi, and their
children were the "jewels" of the same.  The
little miss who became Mrs. Schimmelpenninck
"preferred dining with Scipio to supping with
Lucullus."  The letters written to his mamma by
Master Malkin at the age of five take away one's
breath.  No wonder that he did not survive to
maturity.  Round the portrait—a pretty, winning
face—prefixed to the Memoirs of this intellectual
prodigy, is a design by Blake, engraved by Cromek.
This design is made the occasion of a kindly and
lengthened comment on the works of Blake,
whom Malkin calls an "untutored proficient."

The Cromek whose name is attached to the able copper-plate, and who was much employed in engraving Stothard's book-prints, was a very "canny" Yorkshireman, who had an eye for excellent art and a head for profitable trade. His health was not good and was made worse by application to the graver; he therefore looked out for some way of using the brains of others for his own benefit. For twenty guineas he obtained twelve of the finest of Blake's designs from Blair's poem of *The Grave*. These he submitted to Fuseli, West, Cosway, Flaxman, Lawrence, Nollekens, and Stothard, to Thomas Hope ("Anastatius Hope"), and to Mr. Locke, of Norbury, from each of whom he obtained high testimonials of their excellence. He then engaged Blake to cut them in copper. One or two were executed; but Cromek, who was a pupil of Bartolozzi, whose style of engraving was eminently clear and fascinating to the general eye, felt and felt justly that such an austere rendering would never be relished by the public. He therefore put them into the hands of Lewis Schiavonetti, a native of Bassano, who was a fellow-pupil at Bartolozzi's and surpassed his master. The knowledge and skill, the sense of "grandeur and grace" possessed

by Schiavonetti produced the happiest results.
Mr. Gilchrist says that Cromek "jockeyed Blake
out of his copyright"; and that Blake was
naturally enraged at being supplanted by Schiavonetti and despoiled by Cromek. While *The
Grave* was in the course of execution Blake got
hold of a magnificent subject of which Cromek
had the wit to feel the value.

Out of the whole range of modern literature no
more picturesque, ample, or central theme could
be discovered than the *Canterbury Pilgrimage* of
Chaucer. A fine passage from the hand of the
discoverer of this admirable subject, in what seems
to us the best prose document remaining from his
pen, shows the dignity of the conception : "The
characters of Chaucer's Pilgrims are the characters
which compose all ages and nations. As one age
falls another rises, different to mortal sight, but to
immortals only the same; for we see the same
character repeated again and again in animals,
vegetables, minerals, and in men. Nothing new
occurs in identical existence. Accident ever
varies. Substance can never suffer change or
decay. Of Chaucer's characters, as described in
his *Canterbury Tales*, some of the names or titles
are altered by time, but the characters themselves

for ever remain unaltered; and consequently they
are the physiognomies or lineaments of universal
human life, beyond which Nature never steps.
Names alter, things never alter. I have known
multitudes of those who would have been monks
in the age of monkery, who in this deistical age
are deists. As Newton numbered the stars, and
as Linnæus numbered the plants, so Chaucer
numbered the classes of men."

Some of the individual criticisms in this document seem to us very full of penetration, as, for example : "The Ploughman is simplicity itself, with
wisdom and strength for its stamina. Chaucer has
divided the ancient character of Hercules between
his Miller and his Ploughman. Benevolence is the
Ploughman's great characteristic. He is thin with
excessive labour, and not with old age, as some
have supposed—

> " He woulde thresh and thereto dike and delve,
> For Christe's sake, for every poore wight
> Withouten hire if it lay in his might.

The Ploughman of Chaucer is Hercules in his
supreme eternal state divested of his spectrous
shadow, which is the Miller, a terrible fellow,
such as exists in all times and places for the trial
of men, to astonish every neighbourhood with

brutal strength and courage, to get rich and
powerful to curb the pride of man."

Again, " Read Chaucer's description of the
Good Parson, and bow the head and the knee to
Him who in every age sends us such a burning
and a shining light. Search, O ye rich and
powerful, for these men, and obey their counsel,
then shall the golden age return. But, alas! you
will not easily distinguish him from the Friar and
the Pardoner; they also are 'full solemn men,'
and their counsel you will continue to follow."
These observations seem to look forward to the
days of revived Ritualism, when "full solemn
men" are in danger of obscuring the daylight of
the Good Parson of Chaucer, of whom it is said—

> *The lore of Christ and His Apostles twelve*
> *He taught, but first he followed it himselve.*

The attack on Stothard's rival picture in the
document from which we quote, shows on the one
hand the excited yet stingless and futile sarcasm
of men of Blake's high imaginative organisation.
Mr. Gilchrist truly says: " Angels of light make
sorry wits—handle mere terrestrial weapons of
sarcasm and humorous assault in a very clumsy,
ineffectual manner." Speaking of Stothard's com-

position of the same subject, after pointing out a
variety of inaccuracies, he says : " In this manner
he has jumbled his dumb dollies together, and is
praised by his equals for it."

Cromek endeavoured to purchase Blake's invention for the same purpose as *The Grave*, viz. to
have it separately engraved by Schiavonetti ;
but Blake, smarting under Cromek's treatment,
refused to sell it on those conditions, and issued
a prospectus for an engraving to be done by
himself. Meantime Cromek went to Stothard,
commissioned at the price of sixty guineas a small
oil painting of the same subject, the etching of
which was forwarded by Schiavonetti, and which
was completed by several other hands after the
premature death of that eminent engraver. It
had a great success. The visitor to Abbotsford,
passing through that little romantic study, with
the dark leathern chair where " the Great
Unknown" sat through long years to write his
fictions, and where fancy sees him throwing on the
ground sheet after sheet of that Life of Napoleon
which was done with such marvellous celerity,
will see in a dark broad frame over the fireplace
an impression of this engraving of the *Canterbury
Pilgrimage* after Stothard. It is the only design in

the room.   Sir Walter Scott admired it greatly, but
remarked of the young and graceful Squire that "as
soon as his horse moves he will go over its head."

Cromek does not come well out of this adventure.   As a matter of business our sympathies go
with the wronged inventor twice deprived of the
fruit of his labours, with no powerful friends to
see him · righted, and at that time with no
possible appeal to the law of the land.   There
is a letter printed at full length in the *Biography* which reveals the mind of a mean and
insolent man bent only on his own profit and
aggrandisement.   One sentence is worth quoting
for its virulence : "Why did you so *furiously rage*
at the success of the little picture (Stothard's) of
the *Pilgrimage?*   Three thousand people have
now *seen it and have approved of it.*   Believe me,
yours is *the voice of one crying in the wilderness !* "
Here we have quotations from the Psalms and
from Him who told the publicans to "exact no
more than that which was appointed them," used
to taunt one whom he himself in a former part
of the letter believed to have been "altogether
abstracted from this world, holding communion
with the world of spirits, simple, unoffending—
a combination of the serpent and the dove,"—

flinging in his teeth his sublime helplessness and
the vexation of his own unjust success. Blake
had only the wilderness of neglect wherein to cry,
and the consolation of a few not very malignant
satirical verses in the dear little account-book
on Mr. Rossetti's shelves. Here is one of these
feebly severe couplets—

> Cromek loves artists as he loves his meat :
> He loves the art—but 'tis the art to cheat !

As to the actual result of Cromek's doings on
the fame of Blake, we must say that no more
complete instance of wise and subtle interpretation of the thoughts of another man was ever
given than that by Schiavonetti in the designs
from *The Grave.* Coleridge, in translating Schiller's
*Wallenstein,* founds on two suggestive lines the
noble passage beginning—

> O never rudely will I blame his faith, etc.

And in something of the same spirit of ample
and discerning interpretation did this intelligent
Italian render those noble conceptions so that
they could be understood by the public. There
is no impertinent addition, no unfeeling omission ;
and yet there is a correct elegance superadded
which must win every eye.

The *Canterbury Pilgrimage* of Blake is, we regret to say, on the whole, a failure as to execution in our judgment. The conception and composition are stately and strong. It might be taken from an early fresco in some "Campo Santo." But the horses, which he says "he has varied according to their riders," are so variously like what the Trojan horse might have been, and so liable to be thought like what the less epic rocking-horse usually is; there is such a portrait-like, grim stare on all the faces, such a grotesque and improbable quality about the "Wife of Bath," who is something between a jewelled Hindoo idol and the ugly Madonna of a wayside shrine—that we cannot help feeling how, in spite of a hundred redeeming virtues of strength and grandeur, all the effort in the world would fail to recommend it to the general eye. Yet as a quaint, "most ancient," and delightful ornament for a dim oaken staircase we recommend its acquisition to all who can by any means procure a copy of it.

The designs from Blair's poem were dedicated to the Queen of England as

> What I have borne on solemn wing
> From the vast regions of the grave.

These words are truthful enough.

As the book is more readily to be seen than any other of Blake's works, we will not here speak of them *in extenso*; but we cannot help feeling as we write the wave of that "solemn wing," nor seeing, far stretching into the dimness of oblivion, the sights which Blake unveiled in those "vast regions of the grave": "Kings and counsellors of the earth, which built desolate places for themselves, and princes that had gold, and filled their houses with silver," lying side by side with awful, open gaze, in the dusky silence, waiting for the trumpet of final awaking. Infancy, youth, manhood, and age, trooping hurriedly downward into the bleak darkness and "monumental caves of death." The huge, Herculean struggle of "the wicked strong man" against the victorious, impalpable "shadow with the keys"; the sweet "soul hovering over the body"; the pictured realisation of Burns's tender wish—a family found at last—

No wanderer lost—
A family in heaven.

Above all, that elevating vision worthy of the Sistine roof where Age, "a-leaning on his crutch," is driven by the last stress of the furious tempest of life into the Gate of Death; but where, over-

head, " young and lusty as the eagle," the new-
born, immortal, worshipping man of the skies
kneels in the radiance of the supernal sun of
eternity.   This book was indeed a fit overture to
that still greater oratorio of *Job*, with which, as
if accompanied by a mighty Miltonic organ, the
Master virtually concluded his pictured lays.

It is to the thoughtful and self-denying kindness of the venerable John Linnell that we owe
the production of the *Illustration of the Book of
Job*.   Will it be believed that Blake was nearly
seventy years old when this marvellous series of
designs was commenced?

To show his manner of life at this period, and
his surroundings, we must copy at some length a
minute picture of the occasional visits paid by
him to his friends the Linnells, at Hampstead
Heath, not long before his death—

Blake was at this period in the habit, when well,
of spending frequent happy Sundays at his friend's
Hampstead cottage, where he was received by host
and hostess with the most cordial affection.   Mr.
Linnell's manner was that of a son; Mrs. Linnell was
hospitable and kind, as ladies well know how to be to
a valued friend.   The children, whenever he was expected, were on the *qui vive* to catch the first glimpse

of him from afar.  One of them who has now children
of her own, but still cherishes the old reverence for
"Mr. Blake," remembers thus watching for him when
a little girl of five or six ; and how, as he walked over
the brow of the hill and came within sight of the
young ones, he would make a particular signal ; how
Dr. Thornton, another friend, and frequent visitor,
would make a different one,—the Doctor taking off
his hat and raising it on his stick.  She remembers
how Blake would take her on his knee and recite
children's stories to them all ; recollects his kind
manner ; his putting her in the way of drawing,
training her from his own doings.  One day he
brought up to Hampstead an early sketch-book, full
of most singular things, as it seemed to the children.
But in the midst of them they came upon a finished
pre-Raphaelite-like drawing of a grasshopper, with
which they were delighted.

Mr. Linnell had first taken lodgings at Hampstead
in June 1822, and in March 1824 moved his family
to a farmhouse there, part of which was let off as a
separate habitation—as it is to this day ; for Collins's
Farm yet stands, altered by the erection of new out-
buildings and the loss of some of its trees, but not so
much altered as most things in Hampstead.  It is on
the north or countryward side, beyond the Heath,
between North End and the "Spaniards."  North End,
every cockney knows, lies in a hollow over the Heath,
a cluster of villa residences amid gardens and pleasure-

grounds, their roofs embosomed in trees.   As you walk from it towards the "Spaniards," a winding lane to the left brings you back into the same high road. A little off this there is another winding way, in the middle of which stands Collins's Farm, at the bottom of another hollow.   The house, an old one, looks out in front upon the heathery hillside, at back upon meadows and hedgerows, in summer one monotonous tint of heavy green.   From the hillside the well-pitched red roof of the farmhouse picturesquely peeps out among the trees below.   To London children the place must have been a little Paradise.

Blake, too, notwithstanding a theoretic dislike to Hampstead, practically enjoyed his visits.   Mr. Linnell's part of the house—a later erection than the rest, and of lower height, with a separate entrance through the garden, which stretches beside—was small and humble, containing only five rooms.   In front it commanded a pleasant southern aspect. Blake, it is still remembered, would often stand at the door, gazing in tranquil reverie across the garden toward the gorse-clad hill.   He liked sitting in the arbour at the bottom of the long garden, or walking up and down the same at dusk, while the cows, munching their evening meal, were audible from the farmyard on the other side of the hedge.   He was very fond of hearing Mrs. Linnell sing Scottish songs, and would sit by the pianoforte, tears falling from

his eyes, while he listened to the Border melody to
which the song is set, commencing—

> O Nanny's hair is yellow as gowd,
> And her een as the lift are blue.

To simple national melodies Blake was very im-
pressionable, though not so to music of more complicated structure. He himself still sang in a voice
tremulous with age, sometimes old ballads, sometimes
his own songs to melodies of his own. The modest
interior of the rustic cottage was rendered delightful,
as artists generally can render their houses, by tasteful fitting up and by fine prints and pictures hanging
on the walls. Many an interesting friendly gathering
took place there, comprising often a complete circle
of what are vulgarly called "characters." Sometimes,
for instance, it would be, besides Blake and Mr.
Linnell, Dr. Thornton, John Varley, and his brother,
Cornelius, the latter living still, and well known in
the scientific world, as a man devoted to the ingenious
arts; all, as one of them confessed to me, men "who
did not propose to themselves to be as others," but to
follow out views of their own. Sometimes Mulready
would be of the company; Richter also—a name
familiar to frequenters of the old Water-Colour
Society's Exhibition—who was a fervent disciple of
Emanuel Kant, and very fond of iterating the meta-
physical dogma of the non-existence of matter. . . .

More often the circle at Hampstead would be
Blake, Linnell, and John Varley : a curiously-con-

trasted trio, as an eye-witness reports, to look upon
in animated converse.  Blake, with his quiet manner,
his fine head—broad above, small below ; Varley's
the reverse : Varley stout and heavy, yet active, and
in exuberant spirits—ingenious, diffuse, poetical, eager,
—talking as fast as possible; Linnell original, brilliant,
with strongly-marked character and filial manner
towards Blake, assuming nothing of the patron, for-
bearing to contradict his stories of his visions, etc.,
but trying to make reason out of them.  Varley found
them explicable astrologically, " Sagittarius crossing
Taurus," and the like ; while Blake, on his part,
believed in his friend's astrology to a certain extent.
*He* thought you could oppose and conquer the stars.
A stranger, hearing the three talk of spirits and
astrology in this matter-of-fact way, would have been
mystified.  Varley was a terrible assertor, bearing
down all before him by mere force of loquacity,
though not learned or deeply grounded, or even very
original in his astrology which he had caught up at
second-hand.  But there was stuff in him.  His conversation was powerful ; and by it he exerted a strong
influence on ingenuous minds—a power he lost in his
books.  Writing was an art he had not mastered.

These were the quiet relaxations which Blake
found while the noble plates from *Job* were being
slowly engraved in the little room in Fountain
Court.

Before being permitted to handle its solemn pages, every spectator ought to be forewarned and instructed that these designs are the latest products of a hand growing stiff with age and verging on immortality, and should approach them with something of the reverence with which the young ought to "rise up before the gray hairs." It is true that the drawings for the series were made when he was in the vigour of life. But every line of these plates was cut directly by the patient, wrinkled hand. He was poor, though contented, at this period of life. He had struggled through years of shameful and Bœotian neglect into the valley of age and decline. Even his patron Mr. Butts was alienated from him. The Royal Academy had given him a grant of £25 out of its funds, showing that want was endeavouring to stare him out of countenance. At this juncture John Linnell stepped forward and gave the commission, at his own risk, for the execution of these designs from the *Book of Job*. In pleasant little instalments of from £2 to £3 per week was the simple and frugal Old Master paid, while day by day the sharp graver cut these immortal lines.

At this time he was like a simple Stoic philosopher in his one room in Fountain Court, Strand

(how very strange a place for such a work!—one
would have thought rather they had been graven
among mountains and Druidic cairns), surrounded
by a little band of loving disciples, some of whom
are amongst us at this day—two at least well
known to fame—George Richmond, the eminent
portrait painter, and Samuel Palmer, whose pro-
foundly poetic water-colour landscapes are still to
be seen year by year on the walls of "the Old
Water-Colour Society." *No profits were realised
by the engravings; their sale hardly covering expenses.*

The price of *Paradise Lost* will occur to the
literary reader as he sighs over the last sentence;
but regardless of mere money-success, the old man
ploughed over his last fields as the sun of life stood
red in the horizon, and the vale darkened beneath
his feet.   The "long patience" of this stalwart
son of toil and imagination endured to the end
and saw no earthly reward.   The thin, enduring
furrows of these "inventions," traced by the
ploughshare of his graver, have borne fruit since
then; but not for him nor for her he left
behind.

We must not attempt a full description of
these inventions.   Let us again say, that the style

of their execution is of that intense, primeval,
severe, and unaffected kind most suited to reproduce scenes of the early world, but bare and dry,
and as if centuries had eaten into their substance
and left them as the torrent streams are left among
the barren heights. If with this explanation the
engravings should greatly disappoint the observer,
let him pass by them and go forward to something
more congenial. Their Runic power and pathos
is not for him. Each design has a border, which
is a sort of outlined commentary in harmony with
the subject and often allusive to it.

 It opens with a family picture of the patriarch,
his wife, and children gathered under a vast tree
—the parents sitting, the sons and daughters
kneeling in worship; the " homestead " is seen
beyond close-packed flocks of sheep. Some rams
of the flock and lambs of the fold lie in the foreground, while the great sun sets and the crescent
moon rises over heights stormy and barren. In
the next, the vine and fig-tree of home, angel-
guarded, overshades the luxurious ease of family
love; but above this tender vision is one more
awful. The Ancient of Days (who is to be read
by the instructed eye in His cramped grandeur
rather as an unlettered *symbol* of Divinity than as

a *representation* of Him) sits upon His throne closed in by clouds and bowing cherubim while Satan presents his malignant plea. It is granted; and in the succeeding scenes he works his fiery will. The darkening page seems to crackle with sulphurous and sudden flame; the strong pillars tremble and lurch and fall, crushing the lovely and the strong under their ruins. The rampant, rejoicing demon dances on the cornices and flaps his dragon-wings in glee; while, in the margin, strange glints of issuing claws and eating fires crawl upward. Then the Messengers are seen precipitating themselves one by one on the astonished eye of the patriarch and his wife. In the border Satan walks majestically on the circle of the earth, and round and below him the lightning shivers, "the all-dreaded thunder-stone" explodes, and the billowing waves of fire still curl and creep threateningly. Nevertheless, we see farther on the patient man—still with his attendant angels (so like the angels of Frà Angelico!) relieving the poor as before; but the landscape is bereaved and desolate, and over the sharp stern ridges of the hills the sky encloses another heavenly conclave. The Father of Heaven and His shrinking hosts watch how

Lucifer in his wrath gathers in his hand the bottles of heaven into one pliant orifice, from which he sprinkles plagues and pains on the head of Job. The outline comment shows us the now manifest dragons of the pit with sombre eyes among thorns and piercing swords of flame which are soon to strike through his bones and flesh.

And again, we see the faithful servant of God laid low. There is no vision in the upper air— all is cold and vaporous gloom. The bellying cloud becomes a reservoir of agony, wielded like a huge wine-skin of wrath and poured as before on the overthrown form upon the ground. The sea blackens and the mighty rims of the setting sun seem to depart in protest. The scathed hills and scattered ruins against which the now predominant Adversary rears himself, are abandoned by all blessing, while his unholy feet trample the righteous man into the dust. There is a series of symbols of lament in the border: a broken crook; a restless, complaining grasshopper; the toad and the shard; the thistle and the wounding thorn. Then come the friends, with uplifted hands and sorrowful eyes; while some strange, darting horizon-light like a northern aurora cuts out

into gloomy relief the black mountain, which rises
beyond a city desolate as Tadmor in the wilderness. The patriarch sitting on his dunghill, in
the following design, spreads upward his pleading,
appealing, protesting hands, while the friends bow
beside the dishevelled wife and speak never a
word. Light is withdrawn ; clouds steam from
the rock ; and below, in the border, the dull fungus
spreads its tent where evil dews drip on berries of
poison. Still following down the darkening steps
of grief, we behold the "terror by night"—described
by Eliphaz—transacted in vision over a crouching
group of the bereaved pair and their friends. The
hair of his head stands up, while an apparition,
dignified and ominous, walks arrayed with white
nimbus and fire-darting cloud. Then again Job
kneels, and the six scornful hands of his friends
are levelled against his expanded Neptunian
breast like spears as he proclaims his integrity ;
and worse than this, the fearful, hissing whisper
of the over-tempted wife of his bosom rises to his
ear bidding him to curse God and die.

That is not the extremest depth of his woe.
All hell seems to hurtle over his couch in the
succeeding design ; jointed lightnings splinter
amidst a lurid gloom ; demons throng the

chamber, and shake their chains by the bed;
innumerable tongues of fire search through and
through what should be the place of rest; while
the Arch-Enemy—now transformed into a volu-
minous incubus serpent-wreathed—presses down
in thunderous imminence upon his very soul, as
foul and fiendish arms grasp the limbs of Job,
longing to hurry him away. The border is now
*all fire*, which wavers and soars triumphantly as
over a sacked city. Our memory recalls a fine
stanza, by a friend, which expresses the sentiment
of this dark picture—

> My bones are filled with feverish fire,
> My tongue hath nigh forgot to speak,
> My couch is like a burning pyre,
> My heart throbs wildly e'er it break.
> O God, my God, hear when I pray,
> And help—no other help I know;
> I am full of tossings to and fro
> Unto the dawning of the day.[1]

But now a calm falls on the scene of sorrow.
Heads are uplifted. Elihu, the son of Barachel
the Buzite, speaks, and the vast stars shine around
his head out of the black pall of night. All eyes
rest on him except those of the despairing wife.

There is a listening fear in their regard

---

[1] William Davies, *Songs of a Wayfarer*.

as he speaks, saying, " When He giveth quietness,
who then can make trouble ? "   A lovely marginal
illustration shows, as it were, the beginning of a
new hope.   From the prostrate figure of the saint,
on whose bosom hope seems to lie dead, there is a
gradual lifting up of little angel-thoughts which,
rising higher and higher, at last disappear on their
way to the throne of God.

There follows a subject of amazing grandeur—
God speaks out of the incumbent wreaths of the
whirlwind ; and in the outer space there are
sketchings that seem to represent the very roots
of creation, while its boiling energies appear to
overflow above.   Now the elder sons of God sing
together with clapping wings among the studded
stars ; the Almighty spreads His arms of command
and the coursers of the morning leap forth ; the
silent-rushing dragons of the night issue into its
purple hollows ; and, as it were, hidden in " a
vacant interlunar cave," Job and his friends
behold and meditate on these things.   And again
on other wonders : Behemoth tramps the earth ;
Leviathan wallows in the deep.   Then, farther
on, " Satan falls as lightning from heaven "; the
shadows flee ; the sweet returns of the Divine
favour brighten on the head of Job, while they

flash condemnation on the heads of his sceptical
friends. Still farther, the altar of grateful sacrifice
sends its pyramid of flame into the heaven of
heavens. In the border of this invention are
drawn, curiously enough, a palette and pencils
and a graver. We never see this without surmis-
ing some personal allusion in it and thinking of
George Herbert's poem of *The Flower*—

> Who would have thought my shrivelled heart
>   Could have recovered greenness ?  It was gone
> Quite under ground : as flowers depart
>   To see their mother-root when they have blown,
>       Where they together
>       All the hard weather
> Dead to the world keep house unknown.

> And now in age I bud again,
>   After so many deaths I live and write ;
> I once more smell the dew and rain,
>   *And relish versing.*  O my only Light !
>       It cannot be
>       That I am he
> On whom Thy tempests fell all night !

How sweet and grave is the next chapter of
the story !  Dappled lights break over the newly-
fruited fig-tree ; corn waves in the morning wind.
Subdued, but with more than his old dignity, the
restored patriarch unresentfully and thankfully
receives from " every one a piece of money."

Time flows on, and in future years we look on him once again. In "a chamber of imagery," frescoed round with reminiscences of the long past "days of darkness," Job sits. Three daughters more lovely than those he lost clasp his knees; while he, with longer waving beard and an aspect of deeper eld, recounts the story of his trial and his deliverance, his arms wide floating in grateful joy.

In the last scene of all a full-voiced pæan rises. Under the aged oak, where we saw the former family gathered in prayer, we now see standing in the exultation of praise a group of sons more strong and active, of daughters more beautiful and sweet. The psalm swells on the evening air; resonant harp keeps time with warbling lute; the uplifted silver trumpets peal; the pastoral reed soothes the close-crowding, white-fleeced flocks; a crescent rises as of yore; while the sun, darting its rays to the zenith, sinks over the hills of God who blesses "the latter end of Job more than the beginning."

If we might have our wish, we would select some accessible but far removed quiet vale where Corinthian capitals could never intrude. Here we would have built a strong, enduring, gray-stone,

simple building of one long chamber, lighted from
above.   This chamber should be divided into
niches.   In each niche, and of the size of life,
there should be done in fresco in low tones of
simple, deep colour, one of these grand designs
inlaid in a broad gold flat, which should be incised
in deep brown lines with the sub-signification of
Blake's *Marginalia*.   They should be executed by
men well paid by the Government—men like
G. F. Watts and D. G. Rossetti, and Madox Brown
and Burne-Jones, and W. B. Scott.   At the inner
end of this hall of power there should be a marble
statue of Blake by Woolner—

> His looks commercing with the skies,
> His rapt soul sitting in his eyes.

He should be standing on a rock, its solid strength
overlapped by pale, marmoreal flames, while below
his feet twined gently the "Serpent of Eternity."
The admission should be by ticket—the claim
to life-tickets founded upon a short examination
passed before a "Blake commission."   None who
could not pass this examination satisfactorily
should be admitted to those sacred precincts.
The trees should whisper, the brook should
murmur in the glade for the delectation of those

who had earned their title to enter; and the
lodge-gates, kept by "a decayed historical painter,"
should never open to any who would be likely
to laugh at the "queer little figures up in the
air," which are the symbols of heavenly realities
in the little gray or dark designs we have been
endeavouring to describe.

Some partially finished and very grand and
awful subjects from Dante, also commissioned by
John Linnell, succeeded ; and these lasted in
various stages of completion till the cunning,
patient hand stiffened in death, and the over-
informing mind fled to other regions of existence.

We cannot afford room for gathering up further
traits of character, or narrating other incidents in
his history.   He died on 12th August 1827.   His
wife survived him till the 18th of October 1831,
having subsisted during the years of widowhood
by the judicious, gradual sale of his remaining
drawings and books, befriended and consoled by
a few faithful ones, among whom Mr. and Mrs.
Tatham were conspicuous.   The "Kate," the
details of whose history were so closely inter-
twined with those of her husband's life, to whom she
was so fit a companion, died in Mrs. Tatham's arms.
Mr. Tatham, from whom we remember some years

ago receiving some graphic touches of description of Blake's person and habits, we hope still survives. He painted the portrait of Edward Irving which is so well known by the engraving, and was intimately acquainted with him.

We shall attempt no final summary of Blake's powers and position as an artist. To pay some small tribute to his memory, from whom for many years we have received such unbounded delight and instruction, has been a growing wish; and, in our humble measure, we have been able now to carry it into effect.

He stands, and must always stand, eminently alone. The fountain of thought and knowledge to others, he could never be the head of a school. What is best in him is wholly inimitable. "The fire of God was in him"; and as all through his works this subtle element plays and penetrates, so in all he did and said the ethereal force flamed outward, warming all who knew how to use it aright, scorching or scathing all who came impertinently near to it. He can never be popular in the ordinary sense of the word, write we never so many songs in his praise, simply because the region in which he lived was remote from the common concerns of life, and still more by reason

of the truth of the "mystic sentence" uttered
by his own lips, and once before cited in these
pages—

> *Nor is it possible to thought*
> *A greater than itself to know.*

## III

## ALEXANDER SMITH [1]

THOUGH the habit of reviewing on insufficient
material is to be deprecated, it is not necessary,
when we make our observations on a book which
has interested us, that we should be able to stand
an examination in all the works of the author we
review. The *Last Leaves* of Alexander Smith has
afforded pleasant reading in some holiday hours, and
as it has awakened many thoughts concerning past
impressions of the works of Alexander Smith, and
of the school to which he belonged, a few remarks
will here be offered of a discursive rather than very
seriously critical character. These *Last Leaves* are
interesting, and may be welcomed. They include a
short memoir of Alexander Smith by his friend,

[1] This essay was written as a review of "Last Leaves;
Sketches and Criticisms, by Alexander Smith, edited, with
a Memoir, by P. P. Alexander." It was published in the *London
Quarterly Review*, October 1868.

Patrick Proctor Alexander, who is known by a
volume on *Mill and Carlyle*—the parody on Carlyle being a clever and amusing extravaganza.
There is an oval portrait—taken evidently from
a photograph of the subject of the memoir—a
sturdy, honest face, with beard and moustache, a
solid square brow, over eyes which seem to have a
" cast" in them, not to the extent of being dis-
agreeable, though "there is something about it so
very peculiar." We often see a civil engineer or
a public official with such a physique and such
a walking-stick—a man decisive, direct, good-
humoured, not to be trifled with, putting everything by a touch into its right place. But such a
presence is the last kind of personality which the
youth Byron-and-Shelley-smitten, who turned
down interesting collars in hope of the Muse
alighting on them to whisper fairy-like into his
ear, would have attributed to the chief of what
was called "The Spasmodic School." Music and
passion and self-questioning and the questioning
of the universe are not by the mass of active men
thought to be compatible with hard-headedness;
and yet there are many instances in which they
are met with in close alliance, so close indeed that
the poem is never published, and the "questionings

are all settled by a happy marriage and a prosperous middle age." The great unwritten poems no doubt are more than those which are on record, as "the night of time far exceedeth the day." Poetry is no such speciality as it might appear. Happy he for the most part who can deter himself from turning his poetry into verse, and, above all, who has the fortitude to keep it from the loud acclaim and the fossilising power of the press. Whether this remark applies fairly to *The Life Drama*, is more than we should be desirous of affirming. The public of ten years ago did not think this. Men of middle age will remember when, having passed their exultant youth, they were entering on their golden manhood, while, the mind not yet closed to anything new in the way of imaginative literature, there was a sudden floating into the vacant spaces of its upper skies of a group of starry poets.

*Festus*, and *Balder*, and *The Life Drama*, were themes inexhaustible for young scholars, young barristers, and young ladies of taste and sensibility. Whether their writers were real poets, strong poets, poets whose works would last, was the question. There was a great variety of replies. The younger folk were rapturously de-

lighted; and probably many a now sober-minded
critic first rushed into the field, and threw down
his glove in defence of these lately risen stars.    In
confessing our own position towards them, we
must honestly say that we were not carried off
our feet by the rush.    Whether we really ever
read *The Life Drama*, and *Balder*, and *The
Roman*, in any way giving them a fair hearing,
we dare not at this distance of time undertake
to affirm.    We had voted for Tennyson before
Tennyson was much heard of.   Thin, little, gray
first editions in country libraries had won our
heart; falling on the receptive tenderness of early
youth the silver melodies would not readily turn
out to make room for others.    The *Ode to a
Nightingale*, and *To a Grecian Urn*, and
*Hyperion*, had established themselves in the
memory and imagination, moving reverently round
the granitic and unquestioned monuments of
Chaucer, Spenser, Shakespeare, and Milton, and
the substantial pile which Wordsworth had almost
finished building, and not rudely walking by the
shrines of Byron and Shelley, or disturbing that
schoolboy reverence for the "grassy barrows" of
the elder world, near which we breathed a severer
air, and felt impulses more stately, solemn, and

subdued. We did not, therefore, throw up our cap to greet the newcomers, any more than we received them with a disobliging air. The poet who was "greater than Keats in the very qualities in which Keats is finest," and "whose poems were in no respect inferior to those of the Laureate," did not strike us as being quite *that*. And yet our impression is, that there was in them much beauty and music and pathos and possible power for those who, being on the proper level of age, might have "need of such vanity." And therefore we could, without violently wheeling round, see the sudden eclipse of the rising fame, and to some extent join in the good-humoured laugh created by *Firmilian*. Here, again, we are surprised to find how familiar a thing may, in a sense, become to us without our having gone through the labour of careful perusal.

We should be sorry to commit ourselves to the assertion that we ever properly read *Firmilian*. This, however, we are very sure of, that it was thought very witty, and that it was a "telling hit" against the "Spasmodic School." Wendell Holmes truly says that "society is a strong infusion of books," and but for the staining power of the infusion of that time we should not have been able to enter with so much interest into the volume under notice. We caught the current temper of the hour; helped, no doubt, to pass the catchword which did more harm than the criticism; but, not having been seriously compromised, we can now brush away the unfallen tear as we sigh over these fallen *Last Leaves*, and see how "the whirligig of time brings in his revenges." The brief biography of Alexander Smith is soon told, and another sigh is added by the man who turns aside to see his grave, as he thinks in how small a space is compressed concerning most even able men all we need to know.

He was born at Kilmarnock on the last day of 1829. His father was a pattern designer, who gave him a good education, and brought him up to his own calling. His power and will to *read* was early developed, and in English literature he was "an unusually well-read man even among men professedly literary." The biographer says that it was proposed to educate him for the ministry, but seems to think it no great cause for regret that he did not become "a parson," for that "there seems no special reason to suppose he would have shone as a pulpit orator." The biographer's very cursory glance at the subject, and his view of the nature

III    ALEXANDER SMITH    201

of the disqualification, suggest a wonder as to
what the conception of such a man may be in
regard of a vocation to the Christian ministry.

Alexander Smith did not shine in pattern
designing, but no doubt pursued his work steadily,
writing poems in the interval of business, and
sending them to the "Poets' Corner" of the
*Glasgow Citizen.* In time he forwarded a bundle
of poems to George Gilfillan, who, whatever may
be the depth or strength of his own gifts, had, as
we judged by his criticism of those days met with
here and there, a generous, warm, and enthusiastic
greeting to give to any young poet who showed
reasonable promise of excellence—reminding one
of the fervour and nobility of mind with which
Christopher North wrote his fine rhapsodies of
praise. No wonder that the poet should retain
a grateful sense of the critic's kindness in the
furtherance of his interests at the commencement
of his career. *The Life Drama* appeared first
in the pages of *The Critic,* then accessible to
Gilfillan and his protégés; it was afterwards
separately published, and Alexander Smith "found
himself famous."

One of the pleasant accidents of periodical and
discursive literature is the amber-like power it has

of embalming the "strays" of the world of mind.
In this short memoir of the poet there is an
amusing and graphic sketch of " an original," who,
at this time and as long as he lived, was the most
intimate of the poet's friends.   His name was
Hugh Macdonald.   He was an enthusiastic and
vigorous Celt, who never condescended to English
(though not for want of acquaintance with it), a
factory operative, who by the path of natural
history and poetry—that of poetry being represented chiefly by his reverential regard to Burns
—emerged into a higher level and mixed with
better company than that to which he was born.
It is greatly to the credit of Alexander Smith's
good sense and general strength that he should be
so constant in his attachment to one who in regard
to his poetry could use habitually and unhesita-
tingly such language as the following :—

I like ye weel, Sandy, and that ye weel ken ; but
as for yer *poetry* as ye ca't, I mak' but little o't.   It
*may* be poetry.   I'm no sayin' it is na.   The *creetics*
say it's poetry, an' nae doot *they* suld ken—but it's no
*my* kind o' poetry.   Jist a blatter o' braw words, to
my mind, an' bit whirly-whas they ca' *eemages.*   I can
mak' neither head nor tail o't.

The biographer says—

It became part of the regular programme, at some time or other of the evening, to skilfully lead the conversation up to a discussion of Smith's claims, when Macdonald never failed *in effect* to deliver himself with trenchant emphasis as above, however the tune might be played with lively and ingenious variations. Smith seemed always to enjoy quite as heartily as any one else, what should have been his own discomfiture, and shortly after the two oddly-assorted companions would go off into the night together.

Macdonald wrote songs and sang them in tunes, largely, "of his own composing"; and in knowledge of the habits of birds and insects, the growth of trees and flowers, and in all that lore which is so useful to the poet, he seems to have been deeply versed—reminding one of that strange being belonging to the Emersonian circle, Thoreau, to whom surely the lines in Emerson's *Wood Notes* must refer—

> And such I knew, a forest seer,
> A minstrel of the natural year,
> Foreteller of the vernal ides,
> Wise harbinger of spheres and tides;
> A lover true who knew by heart
> Each joy the mountain dales impart;
> It seemed that nature could not raise
> A plant in any secret place,

In quaking bog, on snowy hill,
Beneath the grass that shades the rill,
Under the snow, beneath the rocks,
In damp fields known to bird and fox ;
But he would come in the very hour
It opened in its virgin bower,
As if a sunbeam showed the place,
And tell its long descended race ;
It seemed as if the breezes brought him,
It seemed as if the sparrows taught him ;
As if by secret sight he knew
Where in far fields the orchis grew.
There are many events in the field
Which are not shown to common eyes ;
But all her shows did nature yield
To please and win this pilgrim wise.
He saw the partridge drum in the woods,
He heard the woodcock's evening hymn,
He found the tawny thrush's broods,
And the shy hawk did wait for him.
What others did at distance hear,
And guessed within the thicket's gloom,
Was showed to this philosopher,
And at his bidding seemed to come.

And, as an instance of this, the succeeding characteristic and, to our mind, beautiful touch of poetic life is worth transcribing. "Once, as we were pacing quietly along a wooded stretch of the river-side, he broke out suddenly, ' Od, but he's a queer fallow that ! ' and, catching on the instant our surprise—no soul being visible in the landscape to whom the remark would apply—he added,

'It's that chiel, Tennyson, I'm speakin' o'. Hark
ye baith noo,' and in his very best English manner
he went on to quote—

> "'Why lingers she to clothe her heart with love,
> Delaying, *as the tender ash delays*
> *To clothe herself when all the woods are green.*

"'Ye mind it, Sandy! it's i' the *Princess.* An'
noo, look ye, *that's* an ash'—pointing with his
staff—'may be ye think it's an elm, Sandy! but
it's no an elm, it's an ash, *an deil a leaf on't;* see
ye na? an a' *the ither trees are oot.* I didna need
ony o' yer Tennysons to tell *me* that—but neither
o' *ye* kent it, I reckon. He's nae poet, I'll aye say
that; but I'se alloo ye'll no aften find him wrang
wi' his flooers, an' his trees, an' things—*he* kens
them, Sandy! an' *ye* dinna. But ye're nae poets,
neither tane nor t'ither o' ye.'" *Indeed,* the poet
of poets to him—Shakespeare, with much reluct-
ance, excepted—was "Rabbie" Burns.

The publication of *The Life Drama,* as has
been said, raised the poet into instant fame; and,
when it is recollected that at the time of its publication he was not more than two-and-twenty, this
was, no doubt, a marvellous achievement. In
estimating the works of men *as* works, we apply
the more abstract standard; but in estimating a

*career*, it is well to pause and remember the circumstances under which the given results are produced. It is true that Alfred Tennyson was young when he first began to publish his verse, but the youthful opportunities of Tennyson far exceeded those of Alexander Smith. An early life of education and leisure in a rural parsonage was passed under the influence of a father, himself a man of great accomplishments and learning.

> The seven elms—the poplars four,
> That stood beside his father's door,

grew in the sweet air of the tranquil wolds where "every sound is sweet," where the doves moan in "firry woodlands," and the brook, with its "matted cress and ribbed sand," winds among anemones and violet-banks—beauties worthily celebrated in his *Ode to Memory*, and not exaggerated by the poet's fancy. He had a college education, and in what company and under what glorious influences let the *Memorials of Arthur Hallam*, and the wonderful threnody of *In Memoriam*, best tell. And yet, when first his silken sail was launched out into the open sea, there were many imperfections seen in the rig of his vessel. "Rusty, Crusty, Christopher," who had an eye for such craft, was able to spy out as many youthful defects as Captain Cap in *The Pathfinder* saw in the vessels of Lake Ontario. Byron was young when he published his *Hours of Idleness;* but he was highborn and was college-bred when they were written, and when his hours were changed by the rod of Brougham into *Hours of Indignation.* So with Shelley. And even from the precociousness of Keats—who was far from being the boy "born over a stable" which the careless phrase would suggest—the "tartarly" *Quarterly* struck out a plentiful mirth—all long since blackened into the merest forgotten tinder. If we remember the town birth, the modest education, the business ties of Alexander Smith, up to the period when, with no large experience of life in any form, he wrote *The Life Drama,* it will greatly modify and guide our appreciation of the native potentialities of the man. That he should not know overmuch of details which hide in the woods, bask in the fields, and glance along the streams, is no wonder, if we have seen Glasgow, and remember that he was designing patterns *there.*

That he should have lifted his eyes to the stars and the sun, and heard the "far seas moan as a single shell" in the ear of his imagination, should

have heard the winds sweep in the wynds of
the manufacturing town, and been haunted by
them, and reproduced them with great effect again
and again, was what might have been expected
from such a youth so born and nurtured.  But the
critics, alas! knew too much and too little.  He
must have been a strong youth to overtop the
influences that surrounded him, and produce a
work which, for a while, constituted a large section
of the critics into a " Spasmodic School " of rapture.
His biographer interjects a happy quotation—

> These violent delights have violent ends,
> And in their triumph die,

as they did ere long.

There seems to be something in the Scottish
genius which gives to it the power of sustaining
the shock of sudden fame more manfully than
the English genius sustains it.  The pleasant
account in Allan Cunningham's *Life of Wilkie* of
the way in which the youth of twenty-one bore
one of the most violent hurricanes of applause
which ever threatened to dash a young painter in
pieces, is worth comparing with the account now
given of the way in which Alexander Smith bore
up under the Parnassian tornado.  The writer

says: "Some little show of elation might here very well have been excused to him, but I should be surprised if any one could say he ever saw in him the smallest trace of such a thing." This fact increases the consideration and respect with which we read anything he produced, and will probably induce many a man, who did not succumb to *The Life Drama* when it first appeared, to return to it with a new light upon its pages, now that the drama of the life of its author is concluded, and

> The monument above his bones,
> And aye-remaining lamps,

are set up and kindled.

One flash in the brief life of personal enjoyment of the results of fame is recorded. He received his first £100, and, on the strength of it, he went with John Nichol to the Lakes and to London, making various literary acquaintance—Herbert Spencer, Lewes, Helps, Miss Martineau, and others.[1]

---

[1] We cannot refrain from singling out a highly amusing note connected with his visit to Miss Martineau. "Miss Martineau, it is otherwise well known, is a little infirm of hearing. When the travellers arrived, several ladies were with her, and by the little circle of petticoats they were received with some *empresse-ment*. Mr. Nichol took up the running, and some little conversation proceeded, Smith, in the racing-phrase, *waiting*. Presently he 'came with a rush,' and observed it 'had been a very fine day'—an unimpeachable and excellent remark which

He also became, for a week, the guest of the Duke
of Argyle at Inveraray Castle. All this was what
any reasonable young poet, of the spasmodic or
any other school, might fairly call success. If he
did not enjoy these two great phases of fame—the
applause of the critics and the favourable personal
regard of the gifted and the ennobled—there was
little of very tangible enjoyment of it to be pro-
cured or expected. He had, and we may hope he
relished, both.

After this interlude, it was needful that he
should turn to consider his future way of life and
" means to live." After a little desultory work
for the press, he obtained the secretaryship to the

brought him instantly into difficulties. Miss Martineau was
at once on the *qui vive*. The poet had made a remark probably
instinct with fine genius, and worthy of the author of *The
Life Drama*. 'Would Mr. Smith be so good as to repeat
what he had said?' Mr. Smith—looking, no doubt, uncom-
monly like an ass—repeated it in somewhat a higher key. Alas!
alas! in vain. The old lady shook her head. 'It was really
*so* annoying, but she did not quite catch it; would Mr. Smith
be *again* so good?' and her hand was at her eager ear. The
unhappy bard, feeling, as he said, in his distress as if suicide
might be the thing, shrieked and again shrieked his little piece
of information—symptoms of ill-suppressed merriment becoming
obvious around him. Finally the old lady's ear-trumpet was
produced, and proceeding to shriek through this instrument, of
which the delicate use was unknown to him, the bard nearly
blew her head off."

Edinburgh University, which he retained till his
death.  The emolument was small (£150 a year),
but it would have sufficed if he had remained
single.  This he did not do.  He married in 1857
a Miss Flora Macdonald, from the Isle of Skye;
settled "at Wardie, near Granton"; and there the
remainder of his quiet life was passed.  His family
increased; his few chosen friends went in and
out; his remaining poems, tales, and essays appeared one after another.  The first splendours
of his fame were obscured by the attack of Aytoun,
and by the laborious assault on his alleged "plagi-
arisms," the work of some one with more memory
than wit, and who surely has regretted the pains
he took since he learned by whom the poems were
written—at what age, and under what circumstances.  A valuable appendix by the biographer
gives a fair consideration to the question, which
ought never to have been so strongly agitated; his
main point being that, to subject rigidly any of
our great modern poets to the same treatment,
would be to expose them to the same frivolous
charge.  Having said thus much, we become conscious that of Alexander Smith's life there is little
more to say.  His means needed more and more
constant replenishing as his expenses increased.

His work—only varied by a yearly visit of a month
to Skye—became more and more close and ex-
hausting.   The daily routine of his post at the
University became yearly more dull and wearisome, till he was disposed to contemplate sheep-
farming in Skye as an alternative.  Then, like Hugh
Miller, as it seems to us, the prey of overwork, he
became at length its victim and died—"a kindly
Scot," loved and lamented by all who knew him.

   The *Last Leaves*, to which the memoir is prefixed, consist of nine essays and two poems,
pleasant to read, and over which we now purpose
to glance.   "Scottish Ballads" is the title of the
first of them.   A slight historic introduction,
picturesquely arranged, shows that the ballads
which have been handed down to arrest the ear
and cause sometimes the eyes to fill with tears,
were not the productions of the troubadour or paid
minstrel of the court or the hall, whose works are
described as being chiefly of the "begging-letter
species," eloquent and witty, but not issuing in
any great pecuniary results.   They got for the
most part as their reward, what the wealthy often
give, so says the *Autocrat of the Breakfast-table*, to
those who are personally hired to amuse them, the
"funny-bone," and had to subsist on it as they

could. The ballads were composed and sung in
the beginning by gaberlunzies who roved the
country, and sometimes by moss-troopers who
reived the farmers of Cumberland, and were preserved, with many intermixtures and interpola-
tions, by the same class of men, who sang old
songs and composed new ones, and were not particular where one began and the other ended; so
that, in effect, like the grand Greek verses, they
were the product of the mind of a class and of
succeeding ages, rather than the single and consummate invention of one genius. The absorbing
sense of personal fame, and the jealous guarding
of "a name," were not so strong on the spirits of
the men of those ages as now. Part of the simplicity and power of the " old masters " of painting
is, no doubt, traceable to the humble habit of
mind which prevented these violent strivings after
personal originality. It was of more importance
that a fine picture should be painted than that the
man whose name was affixed should be accredited
with all the virtue and power of the picture.

Nature worked her will more directly in those
days than in these on the minds of inventors of
poetry. The dreadful swaddling bands of modern
criticism, and the fact that the high places of the

field have been so occupied by the great men who
sang before criticism became predominant, must
greatly prevent that simple, powerful flow of
thought and feeling which makes these pathetic
songs very affecting to us. But God forbid that
we should return to the social conditions out of
which this rude simplicity and headlong pathos
sprang: the burning "peel," the "ranshackled"
homestead, the murdered good-man, mourning
widow, and impaled infant, are a high price to
pay for a vivid account of a raid in verse; and
the weird fairy tales, more entirely pleasing now
that our faith is shaken in the fairies and their
spells, were dearly bought by the widespread
superstitions which brought so many twilight
thrills of fear, and such midnight sweats of horror
and pain. "There is an expression of misery in
these ballads which appears frequently in Scottish
song, and is in some degree peculiar to the
compositions of the nation," says the author.
We are content that our poets should be a little
tied down, if the mind of the peasant may go free
of such groundless shadowy creeds, and the home
of the peaceful farmer be spared the sight of the
seamed visage, battered "sallet," and cruel lance
of "Edom o' Gordon."

In the " Essay on an Old Subject " there is the pensive treatment proper to a consideration of " Old Age."  Cicero and Henry Taylor, Wendell Holmes and Bulwer, have had each to come to their turn over this theme, as most of us have who live to " brush out the first gray hair."  What has struck us in reading most of the essays of the " pensive " kind on this subject, is that to a fair estimate of the question there should go an unflinching survey of *all the conditions* of human existence, the whole destiny and duty of man. Estimated by a merely earthly standard, there is no doubt something to be said as to the ameliorations of the condition of old age.  There is the calmer judgment, the abated passion.  There are the sweet daily habitudes and the fruition which early activities have left.  We much question whether they actually fortify the mind to any great extent, unless there be a basis much deeper than can be arrived at by looking on that which now appears.  An exquisite frank song of Shakespeare speaks nearer the truth in this matter—

> Youth is full of pleasance,
> Age is full of care ;
> Youth like summer brave,

> Age like winter bare ;
> Age, I do abhor thee,
> Youth, I do adore thee.

"We think," said the aged poet, Rogers, "anything beautiful that is young." We have seen and could point to many who seem to have reached a basis on which all the remaining delights of age stand like ivied walls without crumbling or falling, whose heart is as fresh, whose smile as sweetly gay as in youth—but our observation has gone to show that this basis is only reached by descending to a rock not subject to the assaults and mutations of time. The most striking thought and the most important, if it be true, in the essay "On Dreams and Dreaming," is that the dream represents the real man, that disguises and accidental aids fall off from us in sleeping, and that we stand exposed to ourselves. If we find ourselves cowardly when attacked in dreams, we shall be sure to be cowards when attacked with our eyes open, etc. Probably, something of our real character follows us into our dreams. Our life is largely the

> Stuff as dreams are made of.

But referring to our own character on this theory,

we feel a little puzzled. "We are," certainly, at
at least, "seven." And *which* of the seven is our
waking self "it passes the wit of man" to tell.
"Methought 1 was—there is no man can tell
what. Methought I was, and methought I had—
but man is but a patched fool if he will offer to
say what methought I had. I will get Peter
Quince to write a ballad of this dream. It shall
be called Bottom's dream, because it hath no
bottom." The "hempen home-spun," who was
practising in "a wood, near Athens," for the
approaching nuptials of Theseus and Hippolyta,
well describes in these words many of our mental
night-wanderings. At rare intervals we have
what comes nearer to the "clear dream and
solemn vision" of Milton. But when dreams are
most express and clear, there remain the most
bewildering discrepancies. Sometimes we are
charging with the Light Brigade, without the
least fear, and with a full persuasion that the
cannon volleying and thundering vomit forth
apple dumplings; while, at other times, we are
shrinking in craven terror from the stealthy
pursuit of an assassin whom a little boldness
would enable us to overmaster. No interpreter
follows us out into the open plain of waking

thought to tell which of these men is our proper self, and we should be sorry to spend too much time in endeavouring to analyse our character by an instrumentality so variable and vague.

The description of " Mr. Carlyle at Edinburgh " is graphic and most interesting.    To those present at the Rectorial Inaugural Address, the sight must have been as attractive in a personal sense as the vision imagined by Wordsworth, when wishing to have—

> Sight of Proteus rising from the sea,
> And hear old Triton blow his wreathed horn.

Indeed, to the mind's eye, there is not a little resemblance.   Mr. Carlyle's horn is a wreathed and strange instrument, and the sounds it emits as unlike ordinary trumpets as the echoing conch of Neptune is like the cornet of Levy.   We think with most ease and complacency of Carlyle when we try to imagine him to be not a man at all, but Proteus rather, in some of his most uncouth forms ; a shining Arion's dolphin rolling his wet splendours in classic bays ; an Ursa Major tramping the northern solitudes in gloomy silence ; a whale of the Arctic Seas, now diving, as if harpooned, into the gray profound, and now

spouting his "foam fountains," tinged, it might
seem, with his very life-blood, under the piercing
Hyperborean stars. This essay is a tender and
loving description, and not a criticism of Carlyle,
and we must not be tempted to offer contributions
of criticism where, perhaps, the subject is known
widely and well enough. "Winter" is one of
those pictures of a "season" which, issuing from
a hundred pens, never fails to have a subtle
charm, because the seasons as they change "are
but the varied year." The subject is old, yet we
are never satiated ; the red leaf-fall of the coming
winter will be as pathetic as ever; the first snow-
flake as full of wonder; its winds as grand ; its
nights as sublime with stars. And in hundreds of
years to come, the prose-poets will be touching off
the features of future winters as felicitously, the
winds howling as wildly, the streams sealed into a
dumbness as deep as now. The question raised
in the paper on " Literary Work," is the old and
important one of the relation of material to form.
To the apprehension of Alexander Smith the form
is almost everything—

> All thoughts, all passions, all delights,
> Whatever stirs this mortal frame,

settle down upon a few everlasting truths. " I

live; I love; I am happy; I am wretched; I
was once young; I must die; are simple and
commonplace ideas, which no one can claim as
exclusive property; yet out of these has flowed
all the poetry the world knows, and all that it
ever will know." Into which of these foundation
ideas does Milton's description of the rising of
the halls of Pandemonium resolve itself? And
Shakespeare's reproach of Titania by Oberon? At
any rate, the germ is not so precisely *the thing
itself* as to leave no room for the ample operation
of creative force, and variety of material. An
acorn is said to contain the oak, but between the
"towering top" of the lord of the forests, ringing
with "all throats that gurgle sweet," between its
"branchy root," its "hundred rings of years," and
the smooth, green, nut-kernelled plaything of a
child, there is a wide gulf of difference. The
tree destined to withstand the shock of battle and
the fury of Baltic blasts, must become not only
endlessly varied in mode but in substance. It is
this intimate relation of the germinating power and
material to the different forms which it may be
made to assume, that symbolises the exceeding
intricacy of the question of matter or mode in art
or literature.

"The Minister Painter" was the Rev. John
Thomson of Duddingstone, near Edinburgh; he
seems to have fulfilled his functions as a clergyman to the satisfaction of his parishioners, and
also to have made as much at one time as £1800
a year by the sale of his landscapes. With the
moral question of the propriety of blending two
such professions, we are not disposed here to
meddle.

We have long been interested in Thomson's
pictures from an artistic point of view. Living
remote from the modern influence of landscape
art, he wrought upon the old Sir George Beaumont
theory that Nature, if not *actually* like, ought to
be *made* like something between herself and an
old fiddle. He seems to have been stranded
between the two positions. When out in the open
air he tried to make her look like herself; when
finishing indoors he was overpowered by the
Orphean magic of the old fiddle, and it happened,
according to the Scotch song, concerning one who

> Cam' fiddling through the toun,
> And danced awa' wi' the exciseman,

the fiddle danced off with the best part of what
Nature had distilled and measured on to his canvas

out of doors. Yet he had great native power as a
painter. He has always reminded us more or less
of the written landscape of Professor Wilson, with
the exception that there was no "heaviness" in
the touch of Christopher North; but there was
the same aim after a something unutterable—now
gloomy, now sunny—the same obscure and generalised touch—the same eloquent struggle without a
perfect mastery of details. If any of our readers
wish to see a specimen of his work, they will find
one which will give them a respect for Thomson's
aims in the Gallery at South Kensington.

The essay on "Sydney Dobell" is perhaps the
most *significant* in the book. Here we trace an
effort of the maligned and branded "Spasmodic
School" to recover its influence. One of its chiefs,
of course unable and unwilling to defend *himself*,
takes up the cause of another, and with considerable judgment. Ten years have gone by since the
grand assault was made—

> The noise of battle roll'd
> Among the mountains by the winter sea;
> Until King Arthur's table, man by man,
> Had fall'n in Lyonness about their Lord,
> King Arthur.

But the tumult has died down. The scoff and the

sneer are more than half forgotten, and as cautiously as Falstaff—but with more nobility than that "tun of a man," when he ventured to "come up to breathe" on Shrewsbury Field—Sir Lancelot and Sir Bedivere, not so dead as was supposed, look round and whisper to each other, and begin to strap up each other's armour for new warfare. The school—Alexander Smith, at any rate—had behaved wisely in the interim; no clamours or shrieks or revenges had betrayed weakness to bear or to engage.

But the hour comes round at last; and in far less time than it has taken to "rehabilitate" Cromwell and Henry VIII. and Queen Elizabeth, the Spasmodic School are in a fair way of being set on their feet once more.

We have confessed our leanings in regard to *Balder*, *Festus*, and the rest, but must acknowledge that, if opportunity serve, we will "make one of a party" to revise our impressions of at least *The Life Drama* and *Balder*. The quotations given from the works of Sydney Dobell in this essay have had much to do with this magnanimous resolve; and, whatever may be the result of it, we cannot but express our delight and wonder at the exceeding beauty of two of the

fragments quoted here,—one "Amy's Song," the
other a ballad, which we will not refrain from
quoting entire. Its airy music—its rich yet simple
compression of imagery—so ample that a three-
volume novel might be written on its suggestions
—above all, the sense of mystery and awe which
enwrap the listener as its images succeed one
another, and seem to pass off into the moonlight
or sink into the hills like mist, equals anything
of the kind we know. "The earth hath bubbles
as the water hath, and these are of them." Here
it is—

> The murmur of the mourning ghost
>    That keeps the shadowy kine ;
> O, Keith of Ravelston,
>    The sorrows of thy line !
>
> Ravelston, Ravelston,
>    The merry path that leads
> Down the golden morning hill,
>    And thro' the silver meads.
>
> Ravelston, Ravelston,
>    The stile beneath the tree,
> The maid that kept her mother's kine,
>    The song that sang she !
>
> She sang her song, she kept her kine,
>    She sat beneath the thorn,
> When Andrew Keith of Ravelston
>    Rode through the Monday morn.

His henchmen sing, his hawk-bells ring,
   His belted jewels shine ;
O, Keith of Ravelston,
   The sorrows of thy line !

Year after year where Andrew came,.
   Comes evening down the glade,
And still there sits a moonshine ghost,
   Where sat a sunshine maid.

Her misty hair is faint and fair,
   She keeps her shadowy kine ;
O, Keith of Ravelston,
   The sorrows of thy line !

I lay my hand upon the stile ;
   The stile is lone and cold ;
The burnie, that goes babbling by,
   Says nought that can be told.

Yet, stranger, here from year to year,
   She keeps her shadowy kine ;
O, Keith of Ravelston,
   The sorrows of thy line.

Step out three steps where Andrew stood ;
   Why blanch thy cheeks for fear ?
The ancient stile is not alone,
   'Tis not the burn I hear !

She makes her immemorial moan,
   She keeps her shadowy kine ;
O, Keith of Ravelston,
   The sorrows of thy line.

We remember a picture by Dante Rossetti,

Q

called "How They Met Themselves," [1] which
breathes the same mysterious import—and in
Blake and Fuseli there is that something which
sends a thrill of the same nature through the
frame—but it is in such poetry as this that we
perceive the boundary of the two arts and the
superiority of words to deal with the impalpable
and the unseen.

"Essayists Old and New" is one of those
essays upon essayists by an essayist, which gives
one the sort of feeling we have in a room with
mirrors upon opposite walls. It is like what we
understand by breeding "in and in." It is like
looking at the reflected disc of a microscopic lan-
tern, where the queer creatures are seen preying
upon one another, and is as highly amusing.
Where an essayist deals with an essayist departed,
we can more readily receive his comments. For
our own part, the last men we would wish to
review are the living essayists. To be perfectly
fair and just, to speak what we really feel, and yet
to avoid giving pain and provoking hostility which
may so soon be repaid in kind—must no doubt be
a real difficulty. On the other hand, praise comes

[1] It is of a lover and his mistress who meet the shadowy
counterparts of themselves in a wood at eventide.—ED.

awkwardly forth when we remember that we may there also be repaid in kind, and not be quite sure whether we deserve it. Many writers, especially of the essayist class, practically hold the creed of the little Jane Eyre, who, when she was beaten, "struck back again *very hard*"—and though the battle of the frogs and mice is not so terrific as the battles of the gods—it must have great discomforts for the mice and frogs, however amusing it may be to the spectators.

Two poems conclude the volume—one called "A Spring Chanson," with a good deal of beautiful music in it ; the other "Edinburgh," an unfinished piece, intended to be a companion to his former subject of "Glasgow," and containing the raw material of a fine poem.

And now we shall have no more opportunity of glancing over anything from the hand of a brave man of considerable genius, who comported himself well under the two trials of success and attack, and went on to the last with even pace, bating "no jot of heart or hope." Such men—whose advantages of early education and surrounding have not been great—do their best work late in life. The hot-house system of college culture soon discovers and develops the possibilities of

the seedling.  The Tennysons and the Shelleys are
early able to use their native gifts, being provided
with apparatus well prepared by previous centuries
for their service.  But the Alexander Smiths, the
Gerald Masseys, the David Grays, and others have
to learn how raw their raw material is, while the
John Clares must ever remain at a disadvantage.
If, however, health and time be given for development, the nature will often reach its full strength
late in life.  It would do so more frequently but
that the same causes which at first stood in the
way of early culture of a superior order, compel
them afterwards to waste much energy in the mere
procuring of the necessities of life, so that frost
and smoke, blast and blight, gnaw and finally
destroy many a majestic tree.  There is a vast
waste in the great workshop of Nature.  The
Michael Angelo statue heaving through the marble
into awful life is often arrested by an unsuspected
flaw—and genius often

> Finds its own feather in the fatal dart.

So to some extent it was evidently with the
calm and courageous poet and essayist on whose
tomb we lay our little wreath of bays with great
respect, and as we turn the last leaf of his *Last*

*Leaves,* " sorrowing most of all because we shall see
his face no more," let him sing his own requiem
in these verses of " The Spring Chanson "—

> Sing to the spring—but through the spring I look
> And see, when fields are bare, the woodlands pale,
> And hear a sad un-mated red-breast wail
> In beechen russets by a leaden brook.
> For I am tortured by a boding eye,
> That, gazing on the morning's glorious grain,
> Beholds late shreds of fiery sunset stain
> The marble pallor of a western sky.
> Sweet is thy song, oh merle! and sweetly sung
> Thy forefathers in our forefathers' ears ;
> And this—far more than all—the song endears,
> In that it knits the old world with the young.
> Men live and die, the song remains, and when
> I list the passion of thy vernal breath,
> Methinks thou singest best to love and death—
> To happy lovers and to dying men.

# IV

## GERHARD DOW [1]

WHEN a pretty well-informed author is in search
of a simile to express the idea of profound labour
not self-entangled, but issuing in breadth and
power of execution, he will alight sooner or later
on the works of Gerhard Dow. When a half-
informed moralist who knows things by their
names rather than by their essences, wishes to
point the moral of time and skill wasted over
what he considers trivialities, he rakes up the old
story of Gerhard Dow, who spent three days over
a broom-handle and intended to carry it to a
much higher degree of perfection after *that*. The
moralist who, when he takes things by such wrong
handles, has more frequently got hold of a broom-

---

[1] The following paper was published in the *Art Journal*,
April 1881.

stick than of anything more valuable, has not the
wit to see that he is confounding the value of the
thing itself with the value of a representation of
the thing. Yet he knows quite well that he
makes his boast of the two faded leaves drawn, so
very fibrously, by his daughter under the direction of her pre-Raphaelite drawing-master, while
he would tread into the autumnal clay fifty such
real leaves.

Painting is one of "The Humanities." It is
not because the broomstick *is* a broomstick that
we value Gerhard Dow's wonderful reproduction
of it. It is because the great laughing Dutchman,
whose likeness you may see at the National
Gallery whenever you choose, used the dead wood
as Stradivarius used it for the violin of a hundred
years, and made it a phrase in that enduring little
poem in colour for which burgomasters in velvet
and gold have contended, frowning in each other's
broad and glum visages, and which only our
merchant princes or dukes and high-bidding lords
can afford to hold in fee.

There is very little of Gerhard Dow's work to
be had at all for love or money. A street of great
and rich houses, forty-five on a side, with one of
these gems in each, would contain about all that

this notable hand ever did. Unreflective men,
misled by the echo of his name, do not realise this
rarity and preciousness of the works of his order
and school. It is said that Rubens sent out
1600 pictures from his studio (all the heavy work
being, of course, done by assistants and pupils);
Turner, some 2000; and Stothard about the same
number of designs and pictures.

By the aims and peculiar merits of these men
we are led into quite another, and no doubt a
nobler, field of thought. By men like Gerhard
Dow—in addition to such intellectual charms as
his pictures possess, and they are many—we have
a typical world-wide and centuries-long lesson on
the power of labour urged forward and controlled
by a governing and contented mind which loves
its work. If the recollection of the astounding
patience and predominating skill of this man has
not often stimulated the flagging powers and re-
braced the trembling hand of many a student
while pulling through his year-long task, all we
can say is that such students have missed one
great lesson which these works are calculated and
probably intended to afford. To the reply that
labour and skill might have been bestowed on
subjects more worthy of attention than buxom

housewives and their larders and dairies, dead
hares, dinted, brazen ale-stoups, and prize pick-
ling-cabbages, we are not without a longer answer
than we shall here be able to make.

Motley's history of the rise of the Dutch
republic gives us a view of the homely life, the
sweet, pastoral, cleanly industry, out of which
its strength was developed.   We cannot think of
those silvery and golden tranquillities which Cuyp
has set before us, without treading the threshold
of poetic influences as useful in their place as
higher things.   In Tennyson's *Palace of Art*
there were pictures

> fitted to every mood
> And change of the still soul.

Mr. Ruskin tells us with a touching simplicity
how, finding the "weariable imagination over-jaded
among beetling pine-groves and glistering ridges
of snow, he turned with thankfulness and delight
to watch the ways of a tiny colony of ants at his
feet." We do not fully sympathise with Mr.
Ruskin in his want of interest in brass pans.  Let
us dignify if possible the round of the whole day.
Could we but fairly see it, there is a true poetry
of dinner-time.   The glamour of the pen or pencil,

working at the bidding of imagination, can turn a
kitchen into poetry, a housewife's workbox and
wrinkled, thread-scourged piece of bee's-wax into
something more than itself, as in *David Copper-
field*.  Has the wanderer among the dewy Lancashire homesteads never felt the sweet influence
coming from the farm-breathings, and from the
dazzle of those inverted milk-cans, helmeting the
gray posts among the beehives, cans battered like
Prince Edward's armour, and glistening like
Harry Monmouth's casque?  Our appetites are
not accidents, not things to be ashamed of, if kept
in rule.  To the true poet, pea-soup is not without
its distant hint of Helicon.  The water, now
steaming fragrantly with succulent herb and the
sustaining juices of things made for the service of
man, flows, to the illuminated fancy, from the
Castalian fount.  No matter that the poet will
not think so after dinner.  Everything in its
season.  After dinner his gaze will find his
own meanings in the temperate glass, which
will bring before his sunny inner eye the
loaded vine-branches and the flutter of their
golden leaves.

We greatly deprecate, nay, deeply dislike,
those narrowings of the creed of art, those futile

limitations and arbitrary selections which correspond to the shibboleths of society and "caste,"
into which no enjoyments are admitted that do
not come in carriages, perfumed and gloved, and
with an air of *haut ton* about them; or, again,
to those not less littlenesses of conventional culture which the worm-eaten centuries impose on
one particular round of education rather than on
another. Far be it from us to over-exalt the
culinary Muse or to slight or defy the goddess of
the Ægis and the owl, but we do assert, even concerning the kitchen, in a proverb dropped upon
yesterday: *Tous les dieux ne sont pas partis;*
and that as to the reverent eye of the Greek every
corner was haunted by its appropriate genius, so
if there be but given the seeing eye she will
laugh and beam even in the recesses of the
scullery.

A few particularisations of the life of Gerhard
Dow may refresh the memory of the reader. He
was born in Leyden in 1613 and died in 1680.
He was first placed with an engraver, a good
school for learning that patient manipulative care
which afterwards became so exemplified in his
paintings; then with Peter Konwhoorn, a painter
on glass, where he might imbibe a taste for

brilliance and transparency ; and lastly, with the
great Rembrandt, where no doubt he learned to
mingle the keen perception of detail with breadth
of effect and rich impasto. " He bestowed the
greatest care on the preparation of his colours, in
the manufacture, generally his own, of the brushes,
and in keeping his works free from dust. At the
age of thirty years the microscopic style of his
works had entirely spoiled his sight. From that
time he was obliged to use spectacles." These
few facts are about all of any consequence recorded
of Gerhard Dow.

There is not often much to tell of the life of
a painter : his pictures are his life *in extenso*.
Gerhard Dow rose with the lark, we will suppose,
and was " gay and early out"; not to greet the
rising sun, but to watch the market-carts coming
along the flat highways with jingling bells, or to
walk with slow good-humour among the stalls of
the morning market, keen-nostrilled, and loving
the crowded appetising fragrances rising from the
piled abundance of the field and garden. What
poetic perception he had was softly veiled from
himself. He knew and cared not for the name of
poet. To him poetry resolved itself into a simple
instinctive bliss of being. After his hearty break-

fast, over which his white teeth glistened in many
a tempered laugh, he would light that pipe which
he is always charging with tobacco in the portraits
of himself, would lift the little panel upon the
easel, the picture over which three months of toil
had been already expended, and with many silent,
grave puffs would consider what to do next.    Or
he would at once incite and calm his nerves by.
playing wandering voluntaries on the violin, represented in the famous Bridgewater portrait.
Then he would set his palette as neatly as if the
Fräulein genius of the scoured kettle had been at
his elbow, would place his model, a glistening
brown pipkin or a bunch of carrots; then, select-
ing and bringing to a point a fine brush of his
own making, and warning off all intrusion and
all dust, would labour after his "impasto," or
scrape to the ground of the picture to redeem
some lost atom of transparency.    So through the
quiet day, so through the sedate revolving years.
In the evening his patron the burgomaster would
drop in to light a huge pipe bowl and muse with
puffing lips at the newly-introduced pipkin or
the best painted carrot of the bunch.    He would
now and then go for a stroll by the corner where
the quack doctor under his umbrella displayed his

panacea, or peep into the dentist's shop between
crimson globes and apparatus half alchymic.

Gerhard Dow, we venture to conjecture, was
not the man to sketch and jot and long to paint
all he saw.  His mind moved slowly, surely, con-
tentedly, like a Flemish ox.  He never wearied
over the pipkin and the bunch of carrots.  Patient
and plodding as a Dutch dictionary-maker, to
him the painter's paradise was centred in the
beaming, bargaining Frau and her market triumphs.
He painted her face quite as well as he painted
the dinted brass bottle or the soft breast-fur of
the hare.

How strange an influence falls upon us as we
look at this ripe workmanship of the hand long
since crumbled into the dust of the Low Countries!
Well may the owner set such a miracle of thought
and labour as we now recall to our memory in its
cabinet of glass and its rich frame of gold!  It must
have been affecting enough to thousands to set
their eyes on that little oil portrait of Cowper's
mother, the "picture out of Norfolk" shown to
the public some time ago, with no grain of its
tinting gone or faded since the weary, sorrow-
laden eyes of the mourning son rested on them
blessing "the art that can immortalise."  They

would hear his whisper in their very ears, "O
that those lips had language!"  Here is a brighter
picture by a better master surviving in all its two
centuries of bloom, with all its youthful perfections about it; age not having touched it, or, if
touching it at all, only in order to ripen its
charms into a mellower lustre.  A wicker market-
basket is a common homely thing, but look at
its presentment here—every polished, well-used
twig of it following the true undulations of form
and colour, light and shade, through the marvellous patience and skill of the vanished Dutchman
—and see if it does not produce an exquisite
poetic tremor by the thoughts it evolves.  There
is a dead image of the barnyard cock which Mr.
Darwin may compare with the barndoor fowl of
to-day as accurately as if it were photographed.
His once fiery eye is glazed and sightless as a dim
pearl, his neck feathers ruffled, but no longer in
anger or pride; his pale, amber-coloured legs
helplessly and ingloriously reversed, their impatient and masterful scratching among his dames
in the stubble over for ever; the glossy purples,
greens, and blacks of his tail-feathers rising sharp
and delicate out of the speckled hazes of colour
which it required days and days to lay side by

side among the crushed and crowding plumes. "The cock, the horologe of thorpe's light" crows no more to the answering hill-farms. He is destined for the spit of the housewife who holds up the hare. But his fate was glorious, for by what tens of thousands since the year 1650 or thereabout have his perfections been admired and praised. It was worth living for, and, to chanticleer, worth dying for to become the occasion of such a miracle of art. Look also at that purple cabbage, its crisp porphyry, streaked leaves clinging so close together round its appetising heart which yearns for the pickle-tub.

It is one of the joys and rewards of poetry and painting to increase our strong and pleasant associations with the commonest things. Who would suppose a fireman's "sock" (as the pliant, copper-studded water-pipe which is laid down from the main and carried up into blazing houses is called) to have any picturesqueness in it? Perhaps a piece of heavier prose could not be chosen. Yet let those who have seen "The Rescue" tell whether the apotheosis of that dull, dusky, water-soaked, writhing thing did not take place when Millais painted it so well. Did he not in like manner glorify straw and hay in "The

Return of the Dove to the Ark"? And has not
true genius glorified and transformed all that it
has touched; whether Leslie turned the dull ripe
orange-coloured and iron-moulded cheese and
ruddy pippins to poetic account in "The Dinner
at Mr. Page's," and in the sweeter "Perdita"; or
whether, as here, Gerhard Dow threw a glory
over our very pickled cabbage, and "struck a
bliss upon the day," so apt to be a "common
day" to those who refuse to see how lovely all
things are in their place and season?

# V
## POEMS

# THE SOUL'S DEPARTURE[1]

Oh let me die at dawn,
  The stir of living men
Would call my waning spirit back
  Unto its home again.

But at the early light
  Existence seems afar,
Back in the depths of parted time
  As fading planets are.

Let me go forth alone,
  Before the sun uprise,
And meet the springing of the morn
  In its own distant skies.

Yes ! let me die at dawn,
  The stir of living men
Would call my waning spirit back
  Unto its home again.

[1] This and the following poem were printed in *Blackwood's Magazine*, September 1841, under the signature M. M.

## EARLY DAWN—LOVE AND HOPE

So ends the glory of the night,
    So dreary doth the morn appear,
So pale my spirit's waning light,
    So joyless to be lingering here.

Are stars, indeed, but dying fires?
    Is dawn, indeed, so deathly cold?
Gray images of chance desires,
    That perish whilst their leaves unfold?

Is all my soul's unquenchéd love
    But the faint shadow of a dream?
Must all my hopes unstable prove
    Uncertain bubbles of a stream?

Shall all my heart's outgoings back
    Unto their silent stream return—
No mingling waters in their track?
    Dull lesson which with years I learn!

That early light repaireth not
    The ending lustre of the sky;
So sadly fails my forward thought
    I hope, to weep—I love, to die.

Oh, inward, wasting, loving flame
    That warms none other breast than mine,
Which ever burns alone, the same
    In my own being's depths to shine!

Not here affection finds its scope,
   Its heritage is fixed above.
Where shall my heart secure its hope?
   When shall my spirit rest in love?
1841.

## SONG

MAKE bright thy locks and seek the sun,
   Lest home-fed thoughts turn back
To idle words which almost won
   Thy heart into their track.

My soul can never dwell with thee;
   And it were vain to waste
The strength of youth in loving me,
   Whose prime is overcast.

Life glitters on thy perfect brow,
   Thy keen and tender eyes,
As on those chancel windows now
   The glance of evening lies.
1839.

## SONG

Vow no more: I did not think
   Love could die so soon;
Sigh deceit to other maidens
   Underneath the moon:
Sing thy songs beneath their bowers;
Gather them thy choicest flowers.

Weep no more : thy tears are false
    As a morning vapour ;
Write no more thy lays of love
    By thy midnight taper :
Love is fading in my bosom,
Like a rose-tree's scattered blossom.

Yet I thought thou once wast true,
    Even as now I doubt thee ;
I can never smile again
    If I live without thee.
Was the treachery in thy will ?
Dost thou surely love me still ?
1841.


## TO LEUCONOE

### (From Horace, Lib. i. Ode 11)

LEUCONOE, seek not thou to know
    The years the gods reserve to thee,
Nor bid Chaldean numbers show
    The flowing hours awaiting me.

'Twere better we should meet and brave
    The stroke of fate or fortune's shock,
Than count far winters by the wave
    Which wearies on the Tyrrhene rock.

Be wise and pour the oblivious wine ;
    Narrow thy hope and seize thy joy :
One spacious moment now is thine,
    Which fruitless care would quite destroy.


## FROM  HORACE

### (Lib. i. Ode 34)

DUPE of the fool's philosophy,
    For the fool's heaven I spread my sail,
    And prayed cold prayers without avail,
And sent no incense to the sky.

Lo ! fierce across the tranquil blue
    Jove's chariot sped, his white bolt fell,
    Dividing swift the gates of hell,
Brute earth, and wandering waters too.

The roots of shuddering Atlas quake,
    I trembling turn my vagrant prow,
    And hasten back my knee to bow
To Him who thus in thunder spake.

For God can smite the highest down,
    And lift the lowliest from beneath,
    While fortune, strong as love or death,
Gives to the churl the monarch's crown.

### RETROSPECTION

RESTLESS clouds of dusky gray
Fill the sky at shut of day,
Wandering on in solemn hosts,
Flitting dark and purposeless
As a vessel in distress;
Flitting on like unlaid ghosts.

Where the gusty south wind passes,
Bending all the tufted grasses,
Sighing in the bladed sedge
By the moorland water's edge,
Making every bulrush whistle,
Blowing down from every thistle.

On the slope of every hill
Seems to shudder every tree,
Every poplar seems to be
Sighing loud against its will;
Little riplets sweep the river,
Blinding every clear reflection,
Driven in this and that direction
As the curdling waters shiver.

Where the sky has any light,
'Tis a wild and fearful gleam,
Like the spiritual beam

Of the lonely northern night,
Where the muffled sledges go,
Flying shades in wastes of snow.

Not a star can pierce the cover
Where those wide-winged shadows hover;
Nor a note of any bird
When the wind a moment ceases,
And the sand-drifts fall to pieces;
Not a chirrup can be heard.

Oh, how very strange and lonely
To be walking in the meadows,
As a shadow blown with shadows;
As it were a spirit only!

Not a memory of the sun
Crosses the gray waste of thought,
But the silent dead are brought
From their coffins one by one.

He whose voice long since would utter
What thy lips unconscious mutter,
Words of sweet and solemn warning
Spoken till thy heart was stilled,
And ye paced about the field,
Silent in the breezy morning.

He whose steady, strong desire,
Like a slow-consuming fire,
Waited year by year to see
Excellence excelled by thee,

Heart to wish and thought to plan
Noblest destinies for man,
With sublime solicitude,
Yearning for the loftiest good—
Far into the winter's night
Loved to sit and meditate
In the chambers of his mind,
While he listened to the wind,
O'er the spirit's separate state
Weaving chains of argument,
With his earnest eyebrows bent;
Till the mighty issues brought
Stronger faith to purer thought :—
If his disembodied soul
Stood before thee, thou wouldst be
Fearless, while thou saidst, 'Tis he!

She round whom thy arm would twine
When the summer sun was sinking,
And your mutual eyes were drinking,
Thou from hers and she from thine :
All the fragrance of the clover,
And the glimmering hedge-roses,
Closing as the daylight closes,
Come and flood thy memory over;
For the clover and the daisies,
Which the sun unthinking raises,
Seven new springs have blown above her,
She the lost to thee the lover.

# IN THE NIGHT

MANY bells are tolling slow,
Midnight past two hours ago.
Lightly echoing drips the rain;
Ghostly lies the window-pane
Slanting on the shadowy walls
Where the street lamp's radiance falls.
Sleepless, I am staring wide,
Thought and Silence at my side.
Wave the hand but close the lip,
And in floating fellowship
Lead my spirit here and there,
Wavering like a gossamer
Over London dim and vast,
Lengthened street and ample square,
Park and garden, tower and stair,
Spire and dome and creaking mast.
Dreadful London, vast and dim,
What thou art no man can tell,
Brain and sense and reason swim,
Scarcely dare my spirit dwell
On thy mingled heaven and hell—
Scarcely watch
That dark river's quivering lamps
Struggling through its folded damps.

## OBLIVION

OBLIVION claims and equals all
    Of that which was and that which is ;
I hear the distant torrent fall
    And crumble in the dumb abyss.
I see the foaming ages sweep
To perish in the utter deep.

Why, throbbing heart, wilt thou impose
    Thy treasured toil on thankless death,
Who neither aim nor value knows,
    But flings the jewelled drop beneath
The tear-drifts ever plunging down
As rich, as fruitless as thine own ?

For dying ever, ever born,
    Much done and nought accomplishéd,
Man is his own, his fellow's scorn,
    He envies and laments the dead,
And, panting still for something new,
Nought does but *they* were wont to do.

The circuit of the whirling winds
    Scoffs rudely at his vague desires,
Which neither law nor fulness binds,
    Whom the sweet course of nature tires,

Who, where broad rivers greet the sea,
Mourns only their monotony.

Oh, cease thy dread o'er-labouring course,
    Thou myriad-tongued, relentless Time !
My soul is crushed beneath thy force
    Of countless motions raised sublime
Before the view of human thought,
Whose order it inherits not.

Here, stretched upon the mountain grass,
    I see the imperious sun ascend,
And watch the sparkling moments pass,
    As from the giddy zenith tend
Those fiery wheels, till he in haste
Has like a gasping racer passed.

Then anguished in the twilight see,
    With brimming eyes, the lofty sage,
Who watched in deep antiquity
    That sun fulfil his pilgrimage.
His hopes, his tears, with mine the same,
Earth bears no echo of his name.

I bless the dead, whose scattered dust
    Has joined new forms of shifting life ;
I bless the soul escaped its trust,
    Its bonds, its wonder, and its strife ;
Thee, Christ, I bless, who Death o'erthrew,
Whose spirit maketh all things new.

## ASPIRATION

O God, we sigh in Thee to rest,
With life's strange burden much opprest;
For us to be with Christ is best.

Grateful that Thou hast brought us here
Through mists of doubt and dens of fear,
We wait till Thou our Lord appear.

For we would *love*, where love no more
Shall with dark frosts be wrinkled o'er,
Or, lost, in idle channels pour:

For we would know the shapely whole
Which Thou hast given to the soul
For its dominion and control—

The full-orbed mysteries of the sky
Which here in glittering fragments lie,
And all our baby wonderings try:

While now with glee, and now with dread,
In small experiment we tread
Among the living and the dead:

Peering into the daisy's crown,
Until its wonders deep have grown
A mighty gulf to drink us down.

3

5

And, but that wonder speaks of Thee,
How sad, amidst infinity,
With life and death unsolved, to be!

O Life of Life! O Peace unknown!
What though the whole creation groan,
Thou knowest and Thou lov'st Thine own.

And in the solitary place,
Where still and sad Thy suppliant prays,
Thou showest in his soul Thy face:

And to the dusky world unseen
His unchained spirit walks within
In glistering garments, white and clean.

## THE LITTLE POOL

THERE is a little pool in fields remote
(Not many seek it, or admire when found),
Thick set with rushes and broad-bladed flags
In all its creeks among the twisted roots
Of gray old willow-trees; and half-creamed o'er
With pulpy weed, and five-leaved water-flowers;
And in its opening centre, deepening down
Into the fathomless inverted heaven,
Small dwarf-oaks, and the crimpy hazel, shake
On breezy days beside the fragrant thorn
That hems it in; and many a little bird—
Still robin, timorous wren, coquetting finch,

S

Shy blackbird—in among their trembling boughs
Have sung and loved for twenty summers past.
The oxen's lowing is the loudest sound
Heard by this brink, save when, with sudden roar,
The thunder stoops and bellows on the ground
Among the pastures, and its fiery breath
One ghastly instant shows the startled trees
Nodding with terror o'er the blackened wave.
All other sounds are soft and sweet and low;
Light winds pass flute-like all the afternoon
Among the reeds; and wild bees, as they pass
To neighbouring clover, bring their soothing hum
To vibrate in the airs that fan its breast;
The cuckoo, when the days are warm and still,
Comes quietly above, and satisfied
With two plain notes, repeats them o'er and o'er;
While stock-doves, hidden in the dusky firs
Of belting thickets, tremulous reply.
The coot has made her nest within a cove
Guarded by tangled roots and hanging grass,
And he, who in the hot midday will come
Slily across the thistles, there may see
The fleet of four black chicks securely sail
Into that harbour at her bagpipe call—
One plaintive anxious note—herself unseen;
Or, sitting for awhile upon the bank,
May watch the little world of happy life
Beneath and on the surface; down below
The glossy velvet tadpoles wriggle round

The entangled water-weeds, while on the top
Flies, numerous, dart along, or steer across,—
Some in a coat of green and purple mail,
The roving corsairs of their little sea ;
Some trembling on their long, tenacious legs,
Swaying like tiny chariots hung with springs,—
Or spiral troops of ever restless gnats
Whirl round and tease the eye to dizziness.
So full and vital is this nameless pool,
And yet so quiet, that its life might be
Made to portray the tranquil life of thought
Where glittering images sport noiselessly,
And fancies, chased by reason, flutter o'er
The depths through which the heaven of the heart
Lies, the calm reflex of the eternal heaven.


## PARAPHRASE—PSALM XVI.

PRESERVE the soul whose humble trust
    Will never cease to call Thee mine :
The ever Pure, the ever Just,
    Who dost in Thine own lustre shine :
For ever giving ; for Thy store
Flows unreplenished evermore.

How can my goodness profit Thee ?
    And yet my heart like Thine must flow ;
Therefore with those I yearn to be
    Who most resemble Thee below,

That all the rapture of my breast
May spend its floods in outspread rest.


Ah, Lord, Thou only fount of bliss—
    There is no other God beside—
I start with hideous phantasies
    To see the big upheaving tide
Of growing griefs hem in the crowd,
Whose heads at idol shrines are bowed.


Their chalices of foaming gore
    Pressed madly to blaspheming lips,
My shuddering hand shall never pour,
    Unclasped in heathen fellowships;
No name of mystic wickedness
My thankless tongue shall ever bless.


The Lord fulfils my brimming cup:
    He is my tranquil heritage.
'Tis Thou, unseen, who buildest up
    The lot of my advancing age—
Dost mark each pleasant boundary
Wherein my goodly portions lie.


Thee will I bless, whose secret voice,
    In the still midnight counsels me,
And makes my quiet veins rejoice
    With inmost knowledge fresh from Thee

Who stand'st beside me and before,
And mak'st me moveless by Thy power.

Therefore my joys for ever spring ;
    My glory ever triumpheth ;
Though Time's remorseless years will bring
    My flesh into the dust of death,
There will I rest in certain hope
And wait till Thou shalt raise me up.

Whence strike these strange prophetic beams ;
    New powers which I can never tell ?
I see a light that darts and streams
    Up from the hidden deeps of hell ;
I see Thy Holy One arise
From blank corruption to the skies.

Death's unproductive dignity
    Thy soul can never tolerate,
Thou Lord of Life, nor e'er on Thee
    The grave shall shut its mouldering gate ;
Nor suffer God-engendered clay
To melt in its foul arms away.

Show me that radiant, upward road
    To where the urns of joy are full,
Fast by the crystal throne of God,
    Where creeping mists can never dull—
Those fruitful lands that always lie
Girt round with Immortality.

## PARAPHRASE—PSALM XLV.

MERRY heart within me sing,
　　Tune the laughing lyre again,
　　Fluent tongue and flying pen,
Spread the praises of the king.

Fairest, dearest, best beloved,
　　From thy honey-flowing lips
　　Grace or wisdom ever drips,
By the mind of God approved.

O most mighty, gird thy sword,
　　Mount thy white horse pacing high,
　　Clothed with dazzling majesty,
Ride in state before the Lord !

White-robed warrants of success,
　　Meekness, Truth, before thee ride ;
　　But the blade is flashing wide
Which shall every wrong redress.

Keen and swift thine arrows fly
　　In among the serried crowd ;
　　Darkly frowning, scoffing loud,
Smitten through and through they die.

Steadfast crown and sceptre calm
　　Shine upon thy stable throne
　　Built in righteousness alone,
Fragrant with the anointing balm.

Incense rises from thy robe,
 Myrrh and cassia's odorous sighs
 From the ivory palace rise,
Fill the sky and flood the globe.

Bending beauties wreathed and crowned,
 Who on knees of kings were nursed,
 Stand: thy Queen in order first:
Wait thy wish and gird thee round.

Musing while the maidens sing,
 Listen what the voices say:
 "Leave thy lesser loves to-day;
Spread thy beauty to the king."

Tyrian maids bring purple gifts;
 Wealth comes hoping to appease:
 All things crowd thy will to please,
As the coloured pageant shifts.

See the monarch's daughter move
 Splendid soul'd, while Ophir's sheen,
 Ruby, sapphire, topaz keen,
Glisten in the light of love!

Trooping virgins, hymning choirs,
 Pass the lofty palace doors,
 Throng the vast and gleaming floors,
Sing and strike the thrilling lyres.

Fruitful bride, thou wilt not fade ;
   Sons and daughters born to thee
   Sit for ever on thy knee
With thy name immortal made.

*Sept.* 30, 1868.


## PARAPHRASE—JOB XXXVIII.

WHEN down beneath the lowest deep,
   Earth's central mass all formless lay
In swaddling bands of ancient sleep,
   Gigantic whispers far away
Of coming order fanned the brow
   Of Chaos, while the corner-stone
   Was meted out by hands unknown
And mystic plummets, where wast thou ?

When with a vague and golden stream,
   The wondering light gazed softly down ;
When pealed a fresh and awful hymn,
   And heavenly trumpets loudly blown
Rang out from many a shining row
   Of seraphs wheeling round the sphere
   Before the forming of the year—
Before the sunrise, where wast thou ?

Before the ever-murmuring Sea
   Rolled in its first inquietude,
While all its gaping chasms were free
   From gurgling wave and boiling flood,

Shut up behind its dusky bars,
  Unconscious of its human prey,
  Unstained with blood the monster lay,
Nor trembled to the trembling stars,

Where thou? Did ever thy commands
  Give vast effulgence to the morn
When to the expectant shepherd bands
  It rose o'er pastured hills forlorn—
O'er eastern heights of pearly snow,
  O'er budding copse and breathing mead,
  Did heavenly daysprings ever heed,
Or upward at thy bidding go?

Or have thy prying eyeballs seen
  The folded shadows hovering round
Those mournful doors where all within
  Rest in one wide oblivion bound;
Where towering ghosts with stony gaze
  Enwrapped in vital silence stand
  To take thee by thy freezing hand
And lead thee down their darkening ways?

When Winter's wealth of sparkling flakes
  Engendered in the womb of heaven,
Down from its lofty treasury breaks,
  When dews fall soft, when thunder-riven
Wild clouds were shattered in the sky,
  And east winds chase their vagrant bands—

Was it that with thy haughty hands
*Thou* didst lift up thy voice on high?

When was it that thine ordinance
 Wheeled up Orion from the deep,
Or stayed the light entangled dance
 Of Pleiades, who ever keep
Their dreamy watchfires quivering o'er
 The dim abysses of the sky,
 While great Arcturus wanders by,
And slumber broods from shore to shore?

When Summer splits the gasping fields,
 And river shallows noiseless run,
And every herb thy pasture yields
 Lies sick beneath the blinding sun,
Speak thou and stay the sobbing cloud
 In the swollen South that mourns the dearth,
 And send it from the panting earth
To plunge beneath its ocean shroud!

Go, curb yon banded unicorn,
 Soothe those wild asses of the hill;
Go, see the ostrich laugh to scorn
 The javelin'd horseman and his skill;
Go, hold the thundering charger's rein,
 And bid him stand when captain's shout,
 And shuddering clarions round about
With echoes fill the reeling plain!

Bid the strong eagle fan the storm,
  And hawks cleave southward with the wind;
Entrap the vast behemoth's form,
  Or with thy snares his sinews bind;
Pierce thou that strong leviathan
  With spears, his fiery snortings face,
  Or, fierce, his gleaming terrors chase,
And prove the perfect strength of man!

Oh, wilt thou with thy Lord contend,
  Poor fluttering moth which yesterday
Could scarce the filmy barriers rend
  Of that dark chamber where it lay?
Nay, rather hide thee in the dust
  Beneath the eternal might of God,
  Who wields the sceptre, shakes the rod,
And own that all His ways are just.


## A THOUGHT OF GOD

As children dip their fingers in the waves
And feel a shuddering gladness while they see
Their dazzling myriads glitter to the shore,
And hear the wide pervading consonance
That never ceases either night or day,
But fills the hollow caverns of the soul
And makes them sound with vague and wordless
    thought,

That seeks, but never finds, an utterance :
Even so, O Lord, is any thought of Thee.

Like the deep powers that clothe us when the woods
In summer midnights rest beneath their leaves,
When the full moon stands steadfastly in heaven,
And white stars tremble through the blackened firs
Above a steep and gurgling ravine
That throbs with passion of the nightingale,
And strong imaginations lift us up
To float in visions never seen by day :
So wondrous, Lord, is any thought of Thee.

As in the hamlet meadows, while the sun
Sinks through rich elms and humming sycamores,
And gilds the mosses of an ancient oak
Where coos the ring-dove—gilds the chestnut flowers
And turns the countless gnats to sparks of gold,
And pensive flushes o'er the low church tower,
Whence beats the voice of Time in rings of sound
That seem to vanish in eternity :
So sweet, O Lord, is any thought of Thee.

As o'er a vast and blossoming champaign,
Its countless fields, its orchards, and its cots
Lashed round with roses, mounts the gladdening sun
Dancing on every brook and window pane ;
While all at once the woods burst forth in song,
And every flower-bank waves its fragrances,
And early labourers whistle to the morn,

And curly milkmaids sing among the herds,
And every daisy opens wide its cup
To drink the sunbeams and the flashing dews,
And gleaming gossamers sow the earth with light :
So glad, O Lord, are all who think on Thee.

So fathomless, so wondrous, and so sweet,
So glad, O Lord, the thoughts of dying men
Who meditate on Thee amid thy works :
Thou, who didst make the mystery of the soul,
And set therein the mystery of the world,
Teach us to see Thee over, that the abyss
Of craving and unsatisfied desire,
And longings that o'er-arch the firmament,
May rest in widening fulness till the hour
That makes Thy universe complete in Thee.

## QUIET HEARTS

QUIET hearts ye needs must have,
    Ye who dwell beneath His wings,
Though ye carry to the grave
    Common thoughts of common things ;
Though ye into sin were born,
And into the dust return.

For ye nourish in your breast,
    Where no human soul can pry,
Wondrous thoughts of perfect rest
    In a bright Immensity ;

Thoughts that angel vigils keep
While ye work and while ye weep.

But your slow and stammering tongue
    Cannot boast the unuttered calm,
Cannot shape your thought to song,
    Mount nor burn in fiery psalm ;
Scarcely into thought can move
From the quiet depths of Love.

*March* 1854.

## IMMORTAL LOVE

WHO knows the endless wealth of love ?
How far its wingèd odours move ?
When Mary brake with breaking heart
    Her spikenard o'er her Master's head,
She chose, as erst, the better part ;
    Embalmed at once the quick and dead.

We smell on earth its fragrance still,
It curls and wreathes on Zion's hill ;
For as its incense rose sublime,
    From heart and alabaster riven,
It filled the ample house of time,
    And every golden hall of heaven.

## THE HUNDREDFOLD REWARD

(Acts iv. 36, 37)

Joses the Levite paced his acres wide,
Like Isaac in the fields at eventide :
He sowed, he reaped, his long fleeced sheep he
    sheared,
His ox he watered, or his lambs he reared,
And thought, perhaps, to end his simple days
Where cool trees whispered o'er his silent ways.
Time changes all things : other footsteps trod
Those dear possessions of the man of God ;
His heart he gave, and then his land he sold
For Him who pays in coin more rich than gold ;
Through many unknown lands he strayed and
    taught
Of treasures hidden in a field unbought ;
The broken heart he healed, the lost he found,
Opened blind eyes, and stanched the mortal wound,
Cast forth fierce devils, ushered angels in,
Cleared out bright spaces in the wilds of sin :
Then rested in the fields of Asphodel,
Where saints have all, and neither buy nor sell ;
And through all Time's long hours high fame he won,
God's prophet pure, and Consolation's Son.

1868.

## AN ANTIDOTE TO CARE

THINK that the grass upon thy grave is green;
   Think that thou seest thine own empty chair;
   The empty garments thou wast wont to wear;
   The empty room where long thy haunt hath been:
Think that the lane, the meadow, and the wood
   And mountain summit feel thy foot no more,
   Nor the loud thoroughfare, nor sounding shore:
   All mere blank space where thou thyself hast
      stood.
Amid this thought-created silence say
   To thy stripped soul, what am I now and where?
   Then turn and face the petty narrowing care
Which has been gnawing thee for many a day,
   And it will die as dies a wailing breeze
   Lost in the solemn roar of boundless seas.


## THE SERIOUSNESS OF LIFE

SEEING that life is but the Argument
   To the great Book of Immortality;
   That heaven's divine sufficiencies must be
   The expanse of that on which our life is spent,—
But of such only as is finished well;
   How what is well requires both care and pain;

Of what grave wisdom we have need to spell
    That which is true, since only truth can gain
The meed of wisdom—it should give to thought
    The cast of reverent fear: for mirth looks strange
In watchful eyes that mark how being's range
Widens and fills and blooms, as seeds are brought
    From least to greatest by the omnific power
    Which wraps Eternity within an hour.


## THE SINGLE WISH

ONE thing, O Lord, do I desire,
    Withhold not Thou the wish from me,
Which warms me like a secret fire,
    That I, Thy child, may dwell with Thee!

Dwell in Thy house for evermore,
    Thy wondrous beauty to behold,
And make inquiry as of yore,
    Till all Thy will to me is told.

In this pavilion have I hid,
    These many years when hurt by sin,
Or by my angry sorrows chid,
    Or deaf with life's unceasing din.

Blown hither by the blasts of fear,
    Or stooping with the weight of care,
My feet have hastened year on year,
    With psalm of praise or sigh of prayer.

T

Fear tells my heart that I may be
    Some day an alien from Thy door,
May cease Thy lovely face to see,
    And hear Thy whispers nevermore !

This woe hath not befallen yet :
    Shall it, O Rock of Strength, befal ?
Then were my sun for ever set,
    And dropped in that abyss my all !

Tell me this hour shall never come ;
    Plant me so deep Thy Courts among
That I may have my final home,
    And end where I began my song !

*Nov.* 3, 1868.


## MACHPELAH

This small green field, these ancient shadowy trees,
This dim o'er-arching cave, are like a nest
To which my aged senses flee for calm :
Though I have gloried in the open plains,
With boundless distances and mountain bourns ;
And I remember, how in Haran's vales,
When the red evening lay along the west,
We wandered through the palm grove hand in hand ;
I strong, she beauteous, the desire of kings,
We in the summer morns sat by the wells

While the young lambs were bleating, and the air
Was cleft by swallows, and the camel chewed
The cud with musing eye and smiling lip,
While the spouts gurgled, and the troughs were
    filled,
And brown, black-bearded herdsmen sang their
    songs:
For I, too, once was young, and she, my bride,
Went in and out among the milky flocks;
I heard her weave and sing among her maids.
In the bright oasis we pitched our tents,
And when those three strong angels, through the
    heat
Of the white midday came, she seethed the calf,
And bore her seemly till the heavenly voice
Foretold the birth of Isaac; then she laughed—
The doubtful laugh of unbelieving joy:
Yet Isaac laughed upon her aged knees
Whom afterward I raised my knife to slay.
Then princes knew me, and in active years
Life flamed so high within me that I loved
The bright strong intercourse of human things:
But now the unsteady fire of extreme age
Is like a taper held above a cliff
When the loud sea-wind moves toward the land:
Now many voices and tumultuous things
Sore vex my tottering thought and dimming eye.
Therefore, thou Ephron and ye men of Heth,
Give me for gold this many-shadowed cave,

Where, when the stars come out into the heaven,
And the white villages and dusky trees
Send forth no sound upon the brooding night,
I may sit still, and in mid-silence muse,
Waiting the revelations yet unseen ;
For now I walk by faith, and though my eye
Hath seen the sons of God, they come not now.
I seek a country farther than the hills,
Where is their dwelling-place, and look beyond
This complex obscuration of my flesh,
And see the shining of the City of God ;
Or else beholding all that I have lost,
Her who through many, many years was mine,
My heart were like Gomorrah's ghastly stones
Or the blank streets of Admah.   Let me rest :
And with a distant gaze your youths and maids
Shall softly say : There sits old Abraham
Beside his dead, and there he soon will lie.

1854.


## THE REFUGE

LET thought on thought reveal my Lord in me ;
Thou last, best, only, everlasting Rest,
Open Thy loving arms and take me in.
O do not send me unrefreshed away,
Weary and bleeding from my mountain toil—

From the dark hills scared down by howling beasts,
Chased by thin ghosts and doubtful phantasies ;
By dreadful whispers on the lonely height ;
By great abysses full of wavering shade ;
By giant footfalls of my unseen foes.
To Thee, at length, my frighted spirit flies :
Not all the spaces of the Universe,
Whether of matter or immortal Thought,
Hold any hope, or any rest, but Thee :
And Thou art all things to my spacious hope :
Full man unto my weak humanity ;
Full Godhead to my yearning deathless soul.


## ON A GREAT DELIVERANCE

On thundered Pharaoh gaunt and fierce,
    With withered heart and empty hand,
Whose trumpets nevermore shall pierce
    The silence of his stricken land.

He heard the boom of ocean-foam,
    He heard the hum of Israel ;
Nor counted that his doom had come
    On that cloud-darkness as it fell.

*Their* cloud becomes a glittering screen :
    The sea uplifts its monstrous flow ;
Its sands gleam white, and on, between
    Those stately bounds, God's people go.

Cold, silent rose the glacier-wall
  With lilied crest impending o'er,
Whence no foam-blossom dared to fall
  Till their last hoof had gained the shore.

Ah, who could think that God would leave
  Them shuddering by that stormy brim,
And then the incumbent waters cleave
  To lead them forth from Egypt dim !

1854.


## SORROW ON THE SEA

("There is sorrow on the sea ; it cannot be quiet."—JEREMIAH
xlix. 23)

THE moon-drawn Deep, sad, endless font of tears,
Rests never—rests not under mildest suns,
And under softest moonbeams never sleeps.
She sorrowed at her birth, she sorrows still :
Her eyes weep over, and her quivering lip,
Restless with sorrow, whitens round the world :
Now loud, now low, now silent is her voice ;
But still she mourns.   In mute midwinter's frost
Where spiked Auroras crackle in the air,
Sullen and dumb, with white unfooted snows
Wrapt over her, she lies and waits till suns
Of the brief summer crack the icebergs' roots,
While unsealed straits explode, and breaking floes

Heave on black wakening waters round the ship
Whose ribs were clasped all winter in the arms
Of tightening glaciers; then she swells and pants,
And struggles with her weight of turbulent woe,
And welters round the narwhale's wounded sides,
Joining her voice to that loud-sounding horn
Through which his heart's blood spouts into the air;
Or moans, or thunders as the toppling spires
And breaking arches of the ice temples fall.
*Oct.* 4, 1868.

## BLANK VERSE

NOTHING more sweet than this blank rhythmic verse
In which the meditative soul may pour
Its endless musings.   It is like a lane
In the deep rural regions, where the trees
Bend over rustling, casting flickering shades
To cool the way, and wandering up and down
In its mild confines, over hill and dale
It leads by many a gray, milk-scented farm,
Admitting glimpses of its drowsy peace.
Now past the windy, open, heathland goes,
Where lapwings limp, and curlews wheeling cry,
Or where the brimming corn hangs grand and brown,
Speaking of solemn harvests soon to be,
And from some sudden hilltop catching sight

Of rolling woods, or champaign glittering wide :—
Thus on, and on, through all things winds the verse,
Unfettered by perplexities of rhyme,
Or too prosaic reason.   Nought more sweet!

Come then, dear English muse, whoe'er thou art,
Come like a mild, dear daughter of the land,
The land and language that I always love.
Come like an English matron, pure and bright,
Or like an English maiden, frank and fair;
Come with the honeysuckle breath of eve;
Come with the simple wild-rose flush of morn;
Come with no Greek pretension—Russian cold—
Or Persian fever.   Come just as thou art,
Clasped by the loving Present; teach to me
The long, mellifluous, voluntary lay,
Unvexed by hard necessities of sound,
Yet always sensibly subordinate
To one clear music and unshackled law.


## THE PAINTER AND THE POET

For love of beauty, not applause,
The painter in his note-book draws
    A daisy or a thistle :
Some plumy, perishable thing
Beneath gray hedgerows sheltering,
    While March winds rush and whistle.

So by his light and loving line,
Where rapid strength and beauty twine,
   He makes a weed immortal,
Draws forth its soul, transformed by thought,
And leaves the weed, a thing of nought,
   To perish on mind's portal.

Even so the innate poet's eye
Sees comedy and tragedy,
   Stern ode or carol soothing,
Where other folks see none, and he
Stamps beauty and eternity
   On nought or next to nothing.

*Sept.* 15, 1869.

## AN EVENING LANDSCAPE

THE heavy thunderous clouds trail through the sky
With shattered edges, and a smoking shower,
That sends the labourer from the open field
To shed or barn, spins in the curling dust
And passes, drawing forth wide freshening smells
From holt and orchard ; while the sun, blood-red,
Sinks in the wet horizon, through long rifts
Of cold, blue cloud and hazy woods, to rest.
Cuckoo to cuckoo calls from field to field,
And half-grown geese with guttural sibilance

Lie waiting to be housed.  The thrushes' song
Gurgles within the quaint old apple-trees.
Over yon yellow patch of turnip bloom
Stands the white windmill with its resting sail.
The lapwing cries among the tender corn,
And mocks the querulous bleat of tottering lambs
Heard through the hedges.  The white nettle-flower
And the light kex look whiter in the dusk.
The fern-owl twists its note in neighbouring field.
Small night moths have begun their wanderings,
And cross the course of humming cockchafers.
And the late robin at the willow's top
Pipes to its fellow on the poplar bough ;
While mellow thunders, crushing far away
The gathering night-clouds, reach us faintly borne.
And now the hearts of men are stirred with prayer,
The pensive mother lays her babe to rest,
And while the shadowy stillness deepens o'er
The walks and plots seen through the open pane,
Deep wishes crowd upon her, wondering hopes,
Fond recollections, softly trembling fears,
In this hour's pause from labour ; and her heart,
Tossing awhile in its own deeps, looks up
And sees a chasm opening into heaven,
With one high star that glitters on her soul.
Sweet, holy influences descend like dew,
And draw forth incense from her kindling thought ;
Her cares are hushed, her spirit talks with God,
And, in His heavenly place, with Christ she sits.

## THE ROTIFER

WHEN, out in midnight's huge expanse,
  Our gazing orbits stop
On galaxies in braided dance—
  The Sea becomes a drop.

But when, to microscopic ken,
  Life's lessening gulfs lie free,
The inverted wonder turns, and then
  The drop becomes a Sea!

And look! the tideless, shoreless deep,
  Translucent to the eye,
Is charged with vital shapes that keep
  All forms of monarchy.

Behemoth of the small abyss,
  With ribs of glass-like steel—
The force which makes the kingdom his,
  Turns his colossal wheel.

And down a shining vortex slide
  His helpless myriad prey,
Who gathered life from depths that hide,
  Where none could search but they.

And yet, who knows? even there the scale
  Of downward life begins,
Where less leviathans prevail,
  And lesser prey-wheel spins.

O what is great and what is small,
And what the solemn bound
Of great and little, where the *all*,
The *last* of life is found?

To Thee, the ONE—the Infinite—
Is neither large nor less—
Where thundering sun-stars sweep and light
The chasms of nothingness.

Or where, enclosed in globe on globe,
The lessening less descends,
Majestic Being drops her robe,
And Life's last throbbing ends.

Great God! whose day's a thousand years,
Whose thousand years a day,
Pity the doubts, forgive the fears
Which vex me on my way!

Why should I fear, who, wondering, see
Those deeps too small to view?
The Power that made such life to be,
Makes life to feed it, too.

Remembered sparrows, numbered hairs,
Clothed lilies, ravens fed,
Enfranchised spirits—ours and theirs,
The Living and the Dead.

Vast spheres of life—dim shades of death—
  To-day and yesterday—
The vault above—the void beneath—
  Hark what their voices say :—

"No room for fear, no place for care
  That single eye can see,
Opened by faith and purged by prayer,
  And turned and fixed on THEE."

*July* 1868.


## AFTER READING TENNYSON'S
## "IN MEMORIAM"

THEN came the grand cessation of the song,
As of an autumn gale which long has blown,
Bowing the woods and tossing all the streams;
A last majestic gust that leaves the land,
And passes, with deep silence close behind,
Out o'er the seas, and onward to the stars.

1868.


## THE REST

SERVANT, cease thy labour;
Thou hast borne thy burden;
Thou hast done thy task!

In the violent morning,
When the blast was bitter,
And thy fellows sleeping,
Thou wast out and doing,
With thy stubborn ploughshare
Riving up the hillside—
Get thee home and rest!

In the sweltering noonday,
When thy mates were lying
By the purling runnel
In the pleasant shadow,
Thou, with arm wide sweeping,
And with trenchant sickle,
Filledst thy broad bosom
With the tossing corn.

While from highest heaven
To the western sea-rim
Slowly wheeled the great sun,
White, and fierce, and cloudless,
Every blazing moment,
Eager and unresting,
Didst thou clasp the harvest—
Haste thee now to rest!

While the west grew ruddy,
And the birds were chanting
Softly, softly, "Cease ye,
Cease your toil, ye mortals,"

Stook on stook behind thee
Didst thou leave to ripen ;
But thy arm is drooping,
And thine eye is heavy—
Thou shalt work no longer :
Get thee home and slumber,
Get thee to thy rest !

Cross the lengthening shadows
Of the peaceful fir-groves,
Cross the quiet churchyard,
Where the mossy hillocks,
With their folded daisies
And their sleeping lambkins,
All say, " Requiescat,"
Lay thee down beside them,
Till the bells chime to thee,
Simple bells that tell thee,
" Rest thee, rest thee, rest thee,"
Till they bring thee rest !

While the huge moon rises,
And the large white planets
Wheel and glow above thee,
Till the cottage tapers,
Swallowed by the darkness,
Leave no human symbol
Underneath the sky.

Sleep a dreamless slumber,
For thine eye shall never
See the gates of morning
Lift their awful shadows,
Nor the gold and amber
Of the heavenly dayspring
Sparkle on the heather
Of the purple moorland.

Thou shalt wake no more !

*August* 1855.

THE END

*Printed by* R. & R. CLARK, *Edinburgh*

# The Eversley Series.

### Globe 8vo. 5s. each volume.

## Charles Kingsley's Novels and Poems.
WESTWARD HO! 2 Vols.
HYPATIA. 2 Vols.
YEAST. 1 Vol.
ALTON LOCKE. 2 Vols.
TWO YEARS AGO. 2 Vols.
HEREWARD THE WAKE. 2 Vols.
POEMS. 1 Vol.

## John Morley's Collected Works.
In Eleven Vols.
VOLTAIRE. 1 Vol.
ROUSSEAU. 2 Vols.
DIDEROT AND THE ENCYCLOPÆDISTS. 2 Vols.
ON COMPROMISE. 1 Vol.
MISCELLANIES. 2 Vols.
BURKE. 1 Vol.
STUDIES IN LITERATURE. 1 Vol.

## Dean Church's Miscellaneous Writings.
Collected Edition. Six Vols.
MISCELLANEOUS ESSAYS.
DANTE : and other Essays.
ST. ANSELM.
SPENSER.
BACON.
THE OXFORD MOVEMENT.—Twelve Years, 1833-1845.

## Emerson's Collected Works.
Six Vols. With Introduction by JOHN MORLEY.
MISCELLANIES.
ESSAYS.
POEMS.
ENGLISH TRAITS AND REPRESENTATIVE MEN.
THE CONDUCT OF LIFE, AND SOCIETY AND SOLITUDE.
LETTERS AND SOCIAL AIMS.

## Charles Lamb's Collected Works.
Edited, with Introduction and Notes, by the Rev. Canon
AINGER, M.A. Six Vols.
THE ESSAYS OF ELIA.
POEMS, PLAYS, AND MISCELLANEOUS ESSAYS.
MRS. LEICESTER'S SCHOOL, and other Writings.
TALES FROM SHAKESPEARE. By CH. and MARY LAMB.
THE LETTERS OF CHARLES LAMB. 2 Vols.

LIFE OF CHARLES LAMB. By CANON AINGER.

CPSIA information can be obtained
at www.ICGtesting.com
Printed in the USA
LVHW051639241120
672597LV00012B/1428